A Walk through the Prayer Book

The 2019 Book of
Common Prayer Explained

Arnold W. Klukas

Anglican House

Copyright © 2023 Arnold W. Klukas
All rights reserved.
This work is protected under the copyright laws of the US, Canada, the UK, and some ninety other countries. No part of this work may be reproduced or transmitted in any form or by any means, including photocopying and recording, or by any information storage and retrieval system, without written permission from the publisher. Any translation of this work into another language for distribution requires the written permission of the copyright owner, and any such authorized translation is a derivative work in which the copyright owner owns the copyright. All rights are strictly reserved.

ISBN 978-1-7359022-9-6

All Scripture quotations are from The Holy Bible, English Standard Version® (ESV®), copyright © 2001 by Crossway, a publishing ministry of Good News Publishers. Used with permission. All rights reserved. Citations from C.S. Lewis, *Letters to Malcolm, Chiefly on Prayer* (New York: Harcourt, Brace and World, 1963, 1964) pp. 4–5. Henri Nouwen, *Our Greatest Gift: A Meditation on Dying and Caring* (New York: HarperCollins, 1994) pp. 18–19.

Published as part of the KNOWING ANGLICANISM series of books by Anglican House, an imprint of Anglican House Publishers, the registered trade name of Anglican House Media Ministry, Inc., Newport Beach, California. Anglican House is a Ministry Partner of the Anglican Church in North America. Contact us at anglicanhousepublishers.org.

Ellen Kirkland, Publisher Canon Ron Speers, series editor.
Printed in paperback by Amazon KDP

Contents

Part One
Worship: Daily and Sunday

Part Two
The Church: Rites and Resources

Publisher's Note

The "Knowing Anglicanism" series is aimed to provide Anglicans everywhere basic introductions to some of the treasures of the Anglican tradition.

A *Walk through the Prayer Book* is based on the 2019 Book of Common Prayer of the Anglican Church in North America. The ACNA Prayer Book is a member of a family of Prayer Books, classically defined by the Book of Common Prayer (1662) of the Church of England (see Jerusalem Declaration §6).*

The Prayer Book 2019 has been printed by Anglican House in several formats, including a Traditional Language Edition (see www.anglicanhousepublishers.org). The Prayer Book may be downloaded free of charge at https://bcp2019.anglicanchurch. net/index.php/downloads/. It is also partially available in Spanish and Chinese translations.

*For an overview of Anglican Prayer Books, see J. Robert Wright, "The Book of Common Prayer," in *The Wiley-Blackwell Companion to the Anglican Communion* (2013), pages 81–90.

Foreword

This book is a treasure. Akin to all the books in the Knowing Anglicanism Series, *A Walk through the Prayer Book* is written to provide a basic understanding of—a doorway into, if you will—one of the fundamentals of what makes Anglicans "Anglicans." Incisive passages help the reader understand why Anglicans pray from fixed texts.

What is the value of such prayer?

How does such prayer contribute to a personal, living, and dynamic relationship with God?

Is this means of praying the most reliable route to a spiritual life where biblical words, phrases, and truths are "written on the heart" for times when no book is at hand?

The first section of *A Walk through the Prayer Book* focuses on the above questions, and offers practical help with entering into daily and Sunday worship, whether corporate, small group or family, or personal.

The second section leads the reader through all the services and liturgies the Church provides for the life passages of believers.

Dr. Arnold Klukas is both scholar and practitioner. He was professor of Liturgics and Ascetical Theology at Nashotah House Seminary and a key member of the Task Force that produced

The Book of Common Prayer (2019). *He was a parish priest in congregations in London and in Pittsburgh—congregations with far greater spiritual and formational impact than could be contained by parochial boundaries.*

If you desire to understand, and if you have not perhaps even embraced Anglican Christianity, I commend this book to you wholeheartedly.

—The Most Reverend Robert W. Duncan, DD
Archbishop Emeritus of the Anglican Church in North America
Seventh Bishop of Pittsburgh

A Note to the Reader

We Anglicans are "a people of two books." The Bible is the central source of our knowledge of God and what God expects of us. And our highly participatory Book of Common Prayer (BCP) is quite simply "the Bible arranged for public and private worship." More than 90 percent of the text in The Book of Common Prayer 2019 is directly quoted from Scripture, and the rest includes prayers and songs (canticles) that have been used by Christians for most of the last 2000 years.

The Prayer Book brings focus to one's worship of God (individually and corporately) and is also a guide to the Church in its role. No one is expected to read the BCP cover to cover; it is not arranged for that. You will see that Part One pulls together the topics that concern regular daily and Sunday worship into one place. Part Two gathers together the topics concerning the Church, its rites, its psalms, its collects and calendar, and its historic doctrines (formularies). In both parts, the material is arranged in the same sequence you will find in the BCP 2019.

Part One

Worship: Daily and Sunday

Chapter 1

Getting Started

You will soon see the BCP 2019 is a handbook containing various services for worship plus a collection of prayers and Psalms for both public prayers and private devotions. It features many teaching points to help you grow in your relationship with God. Here are some subject entries:

THE DAILY OFFICE These are public worship services, but also extremely helpful forms of Bible study and devotions at home. Through the Daily Office, you can read the entire Bible in one year, or if you like you can space it out to go through it in two years. As a part of these Offices, you get to know the Psalms, which include every human emotion and express every human fear, as well as the Canticles, which are basically song lyrics taken from Scripture. You will learn about the "Church Year" and the ways in which you and your family can celebrate the church seasons as you make your pilgrimage through the calendar.

FAMILY PRAYER This section provides a structure and content for you to use at home with your family. It will teach your children to learn to pray too.

THE GREAT LITANY   This is a powerful tool to use for interceding in prayer for others, and a personal source for inner strength amidst outer confusion in times of personal turmoil or even national trouble.

PASTORAL RITES   These are services that bring spiritual meaning to every major passage along life's journey—from the celebration of a new birth to the burial of a loved one.

RITES OF HEALING   These rites provide not only comfort but also direction prayer and the use of holy oils to anoint those who are sick; the spiritual nourishment of Holy Communion; and the rite of Reconciliation for those who are troubled in conscience.

COLLECTS AND OCCASIONAL PRAYERS   "Collects" include the formal prayers of the Church Year, along wtih many helpful prayers, and are accompanied by a topical index to help you find a prayer to assist you in any given situation.

DOCUMENTARY FOUNDATIONS   The documents at the end of The Book of Common Prayer 2019 explain what the Church believes, as contained in the historic Creeds, the Thirty-Nine Articles of Religion (which were written in 1571 for the newly established Church of England), and some more recent statements, including the Jerusalem Declaration—about what our own Anglican Church in North America (ACNA) stands for.

PUBLIC SERVICES   The services of Holy Communion, Baptism, Marriage, etc., are obviously not intended for private devotion— but if you are married, or contemplating marriage, you'll find much there to help you to grow into being a spouse or parent.

Using This Book

Most of the chapters are arranged in sections designed to provide a clear understanding of each of the sections of the Prayer Book. Thus our basic outline for each chapter in this book is as follows:

PURPOSE   What does this particular rite or text do? Who was it written for?

CHARACTERISTICS   What are the basic components of the service and how do they relate to each other?

BACKGROUND   Where did this rite or text come from? How did it develop over the last 2,000 years?

A WALK THROUGH THE TEXT   Going page-by-page and step-by-step, we look at what happens and why. Difficult words are explained, and the role that a layperson plays within the rite is outlined.

APPLICATION   What does this rite or text mean for me? What are the benefits? How can I assist in this service, or help others to benefit from it?

Chapter 2

About Worship

To begin with, let's take a moment to talk about our whole purpose here. The word "worship" comes from two old English words: "worth," meaning to show love, reverence, and devotion to something or someone, and "ship," an honorific title used to address a distinguished person in authority, for example, Your Lordship. Together they mean the action of showing reverence or devotion to someone who deserves such honor. The Ten Commandments are clear about who or what we can rightfully worship: "I am the Lord your God: You shall have no other gods but me" (BCP 2019, p. 100).

The Anglican Church in North America's Book of Common Prayer 2019 is a wonderful resource for you to use in Sunday worship services and as a real help with your own prayer life at home. In years past, the Book of Common Prayer was often kept on the nightstand or meal table for regular use at home.

Times have changed, and these tables are now more likely to hold your electronic devices and charging station. The way we worship has changed too, along with our culture in the West (and not necessarily for the better either). Our ACNA Prayer Book was developed to help lead North American Anglicans back into the Apostolic Faith—"the faith that was once for all delivered to the saints" (Jude 3).

What does it mean to be a Christian today, and what does it mean to be an Anglican in an ecumenical and global context? What does this imply for how you worship? The weightiness of the answer may surprise you. We are in the midst of another Reformation no less significant than the Reformation that took place in the sixteenth century. A growing hostility to the Christian faith among the general population is forcing believing Christians to band together, both within and outside of the denominational boundaries known to past generations.

We are also caught up in a cultural transformation that links us to other nations and cultures in ever-increasing (and not necessarily good) ways. We are exposed to an expanding multiculturalism that can be enriching but can also seem threatening. We cannot assume that our beliefs and customs are shared by most everyone else. Our own religious beliefs are being challenged by beliefs that contradict ours and by a growing number of non-Christians who have no religious values at all.

Many denominations and local congregations have either retreated into isolation from contemporary culture or surrendered and embraced the prevailing confusion, thus diluting their core values so much that they no longer have anything of value to inform the culture and nothing of significance to say about God.

Andy Crouch, a major player in the contemporary Christian scene, loves the spontaneity of much of the contemporary worship. However, he laments that such services "have a near total lack of any liturgical forms" and show an "uncritical acceptance of pop culture that dumbs down the faith." But he also points out that more traditional worship can be inaccessible to younger generations and is seemingly without enough power to transform people's lives. He concludes that it is not a matter of traditional versus modern tastes; the real issue is what matters to one's heart. He leaves us with three questions we must ask of any form of worship:

Will it be a vehicle for us to encounter God in our worship?

Will it shape us into God's image as He desires?

Will it assist us to see clearly between God's values and the world's values?

Many younger people have been flocking to ACNA churches because they value the foot-bridge back to the Early Church that Anglicanism so richly provides.

The Anglican tradition found in the ACNA BCP 2019 helps us answer many questions. As said before, worship is the *action* of showing reverence or devotion to someone who rightfully deserves the honor; and for a Christian, there can be no other person or object worthy of our worship than God alone. We are used to calling the occasions of corporate worship "services," but worship is not directed toward serving ourselves, but rather toward serving God by the words we use and the actions we take.

Worship is first and foremost a God*ward* activity. We can't give God anything that God doesn't already possess; the only thing we can give to God is our worship—the total giving of ourselves into his service. Anything we "receive" from our worship is only a mild by-product of the reciprocal relationship.

Worship must be in balance horizontally and vertically—horizontally among people and vertically toward God. In contrast, a "revival meeting" is focused on the hearts and minds of the audience and their conversion; it is a horizontal experience with the purpose to create converts. Aimed at the conversion of non-believers, the preaching and music is intended to stir up the emotions of the audience. Bringing people to faith is a good and godly thing to do, but it is not worship in the Anglican sense of the experience.

Once someone comes into a relationship with God, the focus of worship should become a vertical experience. Once we are baptized, we are incorporated into the living Body of Christ, which is his Church. Among our fellow members of the Body, we grow in our knowledge and love of God, and with them learn multiple ways of communicating with God in the service of others. We also learn the language of prayer. As we learn to memorize and internalize the liturgy of the Church, we gain a wide vocabulary through which God will speak to us, and speak to others through us.

Anglican liturgy requires the total engagement of our body, mind, and spirit, which is a very freeing experience. When someone unfamiliar with Anglican worship visits a Holy Communion service for the first time, two things often concern them: we seem to be tied to a book, and we never just sit still; we get up and then sit down, we kneel, and then get up again.

C. S. Lewis addresses both these concerns, as he explains:

Novelty, simply as such, can only have an entertainment value. [Anglicans] don't go to church to be entertained. They go to use the service, or, if you prefer, to enact it. Every service is a structure of acts and words through which we receive a sacrament, or repent, or supplicate, or adore. And it enables us to do these things best—if you like, it "works" best—when, through long familiarity, we don't have to think about it. As long as you notice and have to count the steps, you are not yet dancing but only learning to dance. A good shoe is a shoe you don't notice. Good reading becomes possible when you need not consciously think about eyes, or light, or print, or spelling. The perfect church service would be one we were almost unaware of; our attention would have been on God. But every novelty prevents this. It fixes our attention on the service itself; and thinking about worship is a different thing from worshipping . . . Thus my whole [liturgical] position really boils down to an entreaty for permanence and uniformity. I can make do with almost any kind of service whatever, if only it will stay put. But if each form is snatched away just when I am beginning to feel at home in it, then

I can never make any progress in the art of worship. (Letters to Malcolm, Chiefly on Prayer.)

Because the liturgy has a structure, you don't need to wonder what comes next; and since the texts in the Prayer Book are dialogues, they clearly indicate when you listen and when you respond. With a set prayer, knowing beforehand what will come next, I have nothing to do but to raise my heart and affections to God.

When we seem to have trouble forming our own personal prayers, as we sometimes do, we can turn to the numerous prayers in the BCP 2019 and begin to pray with them; it "primes our pump" and draws us closer to God. Indeed, whenever a Christian prays, even in complete isolation, that Christian is never praying alone; the prayers of the saints from every time and place including the now are *with* that person and *for* that person.

Chapter 3

The Daily Office

(BCP 2019 pp. 11–78)

PURPOSE

Over the centuries, Christians developed a pattern of daily prayer that could be said together with others or prayed entirely on one's own. Remember, however, that a Christian never prays alone but is always praying together with the Communion of Saints, through the intercession of Jesus, by the power and presence of the Holy Spirit.

Many devout Christians think that "real" prayer comes spontaneously, and they look down on written prayers as inauthentic. For example, the Swiss reformer Zwingli would not allow the recitation of the Lord's Prayer in a church service because he thought it would not be coming from the heart. But Jesus's disciples knew the Hebrew Scriptures and prayers by heart. They heard them at their synagogue; it was the only literature available to them. When one has memorized important words or phrases, they are immediately available to the conscious mind—where they also become available to God, who uses them to speak back into our heads and hearts.

Jesus's disciples asked him how and what to pray, so he gave them the Lord's Prayer (Matthew 6: 9–13). Jesus not only taught them to pray, but he also instructed them to offer prayer through his name (John 16:23–24). "Through him then, let us continually offer up a sacrifice of praise to God" (Hebrews 13:15).

Before getting into the subject of this chapter, The Daily Office, let's think about what prayer actually is. Prayer is nothing more and nothing less than a *two-way* communication with God. Because Jesus Christ is the same yesterday and today and forever (Hebrews 13:8), God speaks to us via the Scriptures today just as much as he did in the time of Jesus's disciples. Yet sadly, many people proceed on the basis that prayer is an opportunity for one-way delivery of information to God, such as *petitioning* for themselves, *interceding* for others, and giving *thanks* when prayers are answered. But this totally misses the most important purpose for prayer, which is *adoration* of God for who he is (his glory) and intimacy with God—*two-way* intimacy.

CHARACTERISTICS

For Anglicans, the Daily Office is the beckoning of Christ, calling us into his presence. In the Anglican tradition, over the past five hundred years, the prayers, Psalms, and Scripture readings found in the Daily Office have been the chief means by which we grow into the full stature that God intends for us.

The Book of Common Prayer 2019 is a "workbook" for spiritual growth. There are three devotional contexts that remain unchanged from those of the first Christians.

1. **CORPORATE WORSHIP**   The weekly celebration of the Eucharist, and the recitation of Daily Prayer, which is preferably done with others, offer us fellowship, instruction, and an opportunity to sing and pray familiar

texts that constantly reinforce our memory, so as to comfort and strengthen us when we need that.

2. **GROUP PRAYER**   Informal intimate worship with a small group of believers, in one's own household or in a Bible study or support group, offers us fellowship, support, and encouragement for the challenges of daily living.

3. **PERSONAL PRAYER**   Prayer on one's own, whether spiritual reading, journaling, spontaneous prayer, or silent meditation, frees one from distractions and brings our own personal prayers into the holy presence of the ongoing continual worship of the wider Church.

BACKGROUND

God's self-revelation to humankind did not begin with Jesus. In Genesis, God spoke with the patriarchs (Noah, Abraham, Jacob, and Moses), and thus the children of Israel were brought into a special relationship with God.

The Book of Acts tells us that the Jews of the *diaspora*, that is, the Jews who had been scattered from their ancestral homeland, met in outdoor gatherings and that they had also built synagogues. The first Christians (who were Jews of course) met for the Lord's Supper on Saturday night and gathered again for prayer meetings on Monday, Wednesday, and Friday.

By the sixth century, the Christianizing of Europe had already taken place, and most people were at least nominally Christian. Public prayers were usually held at dawn, noon, and nightfall. The whole assembly sang hymns, canticles, and Psalms between Old Testament and New Testament readings, and public intercessions were offered.

The Great Reformation of the sixteenth century was a drastic change for many laypeople. The growth in the number of educated laypeople, and the invention of the printing press, had enormous impact. Pamphlets were available, and a translation of a German Lutheran devotional book was published in England in 1524. People were being readied to pray in English.

Archbishop Cranmer, the original author the Book of Common Prayer, was a brilliant scholar and linguist, but he was also a man of prayer who wanted the people of England to learn to pray often and to pray well. He reduced the number of daily offices from seven to just two—Morning Prayer and Evening Prayer—and he made both offices very accessible to laypeople, so they could truly participate.

A WALK THROUGH THE DAILY OFFICE

The Daily Office is not a workplace! The word "Office" comes from *officium divinum*, Latin for "divine duty." The Daily Office contains Anglican services that any layperson may lead (except for declaring absolution or bestowing a blessing), and it may be done either alone or in a group. All you need is a Bible and the Prayer Book.

There are several offices. You may think of them as the longer offices of Morning Prayer and Evening Prayer and the shorter offices of Family Prayer, Midday Prayer, and (before retiring at night) the office of Compline. Of course, you're not expected do them all in the same day. The important thing is to establish a pattern you can sustain, e.g., doing Morning Prayer and/or Evening Prayer, and adding from the other offices when you can do so.

Morning Prayer and Evening Prayer have the same structure—with the only exception that the lessons, Psalms, and canticles change in succession. It is helpful to read the small italic directions (called *rubrics*) that tell what to do next as you're going along.

We will now walk through the longer offices. Remember, the organization is the same for both office types.

THE OPENING SENTENCE OF SCRIPTURE   These act as a call to be prepared for worship. You may read one from among those on p. 11. (The ones on pp. 27–29 and 54–56 are organized by the liturgical seasons of the year.)

THE CONFESSION OF SIN   Confession is an appropriate beginning to any act of worship. We need to let go of anything that may be standing between God and ourselves. The confession has been in the BCP since 1552 and is a classic of Anglican devotion. There follows an absolution for a priest to say, and a declaration that anyone can say. If you read both Morning Prayer and Evening Prayer, you may omit the Confession in either of the offices.

THE INVITATORY   The Invitatory *invites* us into God's presence with scriptural phrases: "O Lord, open our lips" is from Psalm 51:15, and the Trinitarian focus of this short doxology "and our mouth shall show forth your praise" reminds us that we are present before the Holy Trinity.

THE FIRST CANTICLE   The word "canticle" means "little song for worship." Several canticles, such as the *Venite* and the *Jubilate,* are actually Psalms (Psalm 95 and 100, respectively). Other canticles are from Scripture, and all have Latin names dating from their continual use in ages past.

THE PSALMS APPOINTED   The Psalms may follow Cranmer's ordering (shown on BCP 2019 p. 735), which takes you through the whole Psalter in one month. Or you can choose the Psalms listed by topic on p. 269.

The *Gloria Patri* ("Glory be to the Father, and to the Son, and to the Holy Spirit . . .") by long-standing custom is placed at the end of a Psalm or set of Psalms as a way of making it very clear that the poetry of the Psalms reflects words spoken by Christ and spoken through Christ.

THE FIRST LESSON The first lesson (reading) is from the Old Testament.

THE SECOND CANTICLE The Old Testament reading is usually followed by a canticle also from the Old Testament, the only exception being the *Te Deum* ("We Praise You O God") on feast days. At Evening Prayer, the *Magnificat* (The Song of Mary from Luke 1:46–55) is always said or sung.

THE SECOND LESSON The second lesson is a reading from the New Testament, and is always followed by the third canticle. Another Scripture song may be recited. At Morning Prayer the traditional canticle is *Benedictus*, the Song of Zechariah, first spoken at the birth of John the Baptist, patron of the Anglican Church of North America.

THE APOSTLES' CREED The Creed may be said once each day or at both offices. Organized in three sections, one for each Person of the Trinity, the Apostles' Creed remains the most concise of the three creeds (the others are the Nicene and Athanasian).

THE PRAYERS APPOINTED The leader invites the assembly to pray, then leads the *Kyrie* (Greek: "Lord have mercy") and the Lord's Prayer. The responsive prayers following the Lord's Prayer are of ancient origin and go back to the sixth century.

THE COLLECT OF THE DAY To begin with, you should know about the collects—just what they are and why they are so beneficial for Anglicans. A collect is a prayer that is meant to gather up the desires of the people and focus them into a succinct prayer. The Collect for Grace in its traditional form goes this way:

> O Lord, our heavenly Father, Almighty and everlasting God, who
> hast safely brought us to the beginning of this day; defend us in
> the same with thy mighty power; and grant that this day we
> fall into no sin, neither run into any kind of danger; but that
> all our doings, being ordered by thy governance, may be holy
> and righteous in thy sight.
> Through Jesus Christ our Lord. Amen.

The daily Collects begin on BCP 2019 p. 22. The Collects for the Christian Year are found at BCP 2019 pp. 598–623. It is customary to pray the Collect for Peace and the Collect for Grace every day. Morning Prayer and Evening Prayer conclude with the General Thanksgiving, the Prayer of St. Chrysostom, and one of four Blessings.

When known by heart, the General Thanksgiving is a readily available spiritual help whenever and wherever you may be. Indeed it doesn't take much to memorize the Collect for Grace and the General Thanksgiving. When you do, you will have the finest of armor available whether waking or sleeping.

The Shorter Offices

MIDDAY PRAYER   Midday Prayer is found between Morning and Evening Prayer. It begins with "O God, make speed to save us . . ." and continues with a choice of four Psalms appropriate to noontime (119, 121, 124, or 126). It continues with a short Bible verse before ending with the Lord's Prayer and a choice of four collects. Its brevity encourages use with companions from the workplace or school.

COMPLINE The word comes from Latin, meaning "the completion of the waking day." Compline follows ancient precedent in its use of Confession, one of four Psalms appropriate to nighttime (4, 31:1-6, 91, and 134), a brief Bible verse followed by prayers, and ending with the *Nunc Dimittis* canticle ("Lord, now let your servant depart in peace . . ."). This is a blessed way to retire at night.

FAMILY PRAYER Although intended for all families, Family Prayer is particularly appropriate for those having young children. The note "Concerning Family Prayer" on BCP 2019 p. 66 can help you get started using the office. Family Prayer is divided into four sections, any one or more of which may be prayed—IN THE MORNING, AT MIDDAY, IN THE EARLY EVENING, AND AT THE CLOSE OF DAY.

Chapter 4

The Canticles

(BCP 2019 pp. 79–88)

PURPOSE

A Canticle is a song that has words from the Bible to be used in our liturgy. The words may be sung, chanted, or just said aloud. For example, samples from the Daily Offices are the *Te Deum Laudamus,* "We praise thee, O God, we acknowledge thee to be the Lord . . ." or the *Benedictus,* "Blessed be the Lord God of Israel, for he has visited and redeemed his people . . ." (In contrast, a *hymn* is a composition that may be consistent with God's Word but isn't necessarily quoted directly from Scripture.)

St. Paul says in Colossians 3:16, "Let the word of Christ dwell in you richly, teaching and admonishing one another in all wisdom, singing psalms and hymns and spiritual songs." Consistent with this admonition, the BCP 2019 has stayed close to the Bible in its choice of Canticles.

CHARACTERISTICS

There are three types of Canticles: New Testament, Old Testament, and "polyglot" canticles (a mixture of verses).

NEW TESTAMENT CANTICLES that have been used in daily prayer for 1,500 years include texts from Luke's Gospel. Samples are the *Magnificat* (Luke 1:46–55) and *Nunc Dimittis* (Luke 2:29–32). More recent New Testament canticles have been added in most twenty-first century prayer books, for example the *Song of the Redeemed* (Revelation 15:3–4) and the *Song to the Lamb* (Revelation 4:11 to 5:9–14). A recent addition is *Christ Our Passover* (1 Corinthians 5:7–8, 15: 20–23, and Romans 6:9–11).

OLD TESTAMENT CANTICLES come from the Pentateuch—*The Song of Moses* (Exodus 15), from the prophet Isaiah—*Surely It is God Who Saves Me* (12:2–6), *Seek the Lord* (55:6–11), and *Arise, Shine* (60:1–19), and from the Psalms (67,95,98, and 100). Two canticles come from the Old Testament Apocrypha—*The Prayer of Manasseh* and *The Song of the Three Young Men*.

Several Psalms are also used as Old Testament canticles, especially Psalms 67, 95, 98, and 100.

Over the centuries, POLYGLOT CANTICLES have developed as generations came to link together diverse Scriptural verses into a unified song; for example, the *Gloria In Excelsis* and the *Te Deum Laudamus*.

A WALK THROUGH THE CANTICLES

Morning Prayer and Evening Prayer have three canticles each, while Compline has only one. These are found throughout the Daily Offices. Ten additional canticles are found on pp. 79–88. They have subtitles that suggest the occasions or seasons of the Church Year when they would be most appropriate.

APPLICATION

As we've said before, prayer should be a two-way conversation with God. We need to learn a language by which God talks to us. The Psalms and Canticles provide us such a language—one by which we can speak to God and hear his voice. But how does this actually work in our lives?

Every emotion known to human beings (anger, fear, hatred, love, vengeance, joy, despair) are to be found in many places in the Psalms and in the Canticles. They even allow us the freedom to be angry at God—by using his own words! Poetry and songs are far more memorable than prose; and the more you say or sing God's songs, the more phrases and images God can then use to connect with you.

Morning Prayer and Evening Prayer are great places to begin a daily habit of reading a lesson from Scripture, a Psalm, and a Canticle. If a verse strikes you as a direct message, stop and listen! Most importantly, be mindful that Scripture is best understood when you read it slowly, even out loud if possible. Doing this keeps your mind from wandering; and it allows God's voice to enter more deeply into your mind and soul.

Chapter 5

The Great Litany and Decalogue

(BCP 2019 pp. 91–101)

PURINPOSE

Litanies were born out of calamity. Often done outdoors in procession, people burdened by tragedy or impending conflict have put all their effort into asking God for guidance and deliverance. Each petition shouted to God ended with "Deliver us, good Lord!" Every edition of the Prayer Book since 1549 has retained the Great Litany because it is so perfectly suited to "Who we are and the One we need."

CHARACTERISTICS

The word "Litany" comes from the Greek *litania*, which means an urgent supplication to a king or a god. The Great Litany is meant to be prayed responsively. It is divided into these sections:

> INVOCATION of the Name of the Triune God and response: "Have mercy upon us."

DEPRECATIONS are confessions of sin and prayers against evil with the response: "Spare us, good Lord" and "Good Lord, deliver us."

OBSECRATIONS: These three clauses appeal for deliverance "by," i.e., on the basis of, Christ's saving work.

PETITIONS: Our several requests followed by the words, "We beseech you to hear us, good Lord."

BACKGROUND

Very few changes have been made in the Great Litany over the many editions of the Prayer Book. Such litanies were common public events in both the Eastern and Western churches since the tenth century.

A WALK THROUGH THE GREAT LITANY

The rubrics (instructions) for The Great Litany in the BCP 2019 state that it should be said kneeling unless it is sung or said in procession. The twenty-eight petitions in the Litany are comprehensive: for the needs of the Church, for human needs, for God's grace to be bestowed upon all people, for governments, the armed forces, and for those who seek to serve and save others.

APPLICATION

Because the Great Litany is for "occasions of solemn and comprehensive entreaty," it is not something that most congregations use with any regularity. But it can also be used for Rogation Days (which are days related to agriculture and industry) and

Ember Days set apart for fasting, abstinence, and prayer. Lent is also a good time to use it, as well as for intercessory prayer when you stand in the gap between God's mercy and someone's need. If sometimes you have trouble staying on track when you pray, the Litany is an outline you can go back to when your thoughts have wandered.

The Decalogue

The Decalogue is simply the Ten Commandments set in the form of a litany. The book of Deuteronomy (5:6–21) and the book of Exodus (20:2–17) each list the Ten Commandments that were given to Moses and the people of Israel on Mount Sinai.

The liturgies for Baptism and Confirmation both stress that a practicing Christian should know at least three things by heart: the Lord's Prayer, the Apostles' Creed, and the Decalogue. The repeated use of the Decalogue in worship is intended to encourage *internalizing* the Commandments so that they are always there for us in times of temptation.

Chapter 6

The Holy Eucharist:
The Liturgy of the Word

(BPC 2019 pp. 105–114 or 123–131)

PURPOSE

We come now to the Lord's Supper or Holy Communion, commonly called the Holy Eucharist. While the word "liturgy" can be used for any text of worship, it often specifies this service or rite. It can also refer to the two main parts of the service: the Liturgy of the Word and the Liturgy of the Table.

Historically, Anglicans have identified the Eucharist as one of two sacraments ordained by Christ as "an outward and visible sign of an inward and spiritual grace." God gives us this outward, visible sign as a means by which we receive the inner grace and as tangible assurance that we do in fact receive it. Thus, the purpose of the Eucharist is to encounter Jesus in the breaking of the bread—all of it in the context of a meal that represents our own personal participation in his Last Supper and our anticipation of joining him in the wedding banquet of the Lamb (Revelation 19:9).

CHARACTERISTICS

The Last Supper of Jesus with his disciples, recorded in the three synoptic gospels, is the origin of all the diverse rites that Christians do "in remembrance" of him. The variety of names these services have received over two thousand years illustrates this: "the breaking of bread," the Lord's Supper, the Holy Communion, the "Sacrifice of the Mass," the Eucharist, the Divine Liturgy. All these have two things in common: all use bread and wine, and all use the words that Jesus spoke over these elements.

BACKGROUND

As we have already said, the Eucharist requires the Word to be read and preached, and the elements of bread and wine to be blessed and given. We do not know exactly what happened at the Last Supper, but Matthew, Mark, and Luke all agree that there was praying, singing, teaching, and a meal, which would have begun with a blessing and breaking of the loaf. At the end of a meal, a final benediction was made over the cup of wine, and a hope expressed as Jews that at their next meal they would be together in Jerusalem. Jesus, however, changed the usual hope to identify himself as the Paschal Lamb, and that he was offering himself as the blood of the New Covenant.

The first post-Resurrection meal of Jesus with some of his followers was at Emmaus, as recorded in the Gospel of Luke 24: 13–36. Jesus walked with two disciples who were forlorn because of the Crucifixion. He explained what the Scriptures said about himself, but they had not recognized that it was actually Jesus walking with them. They invited him to stay with them and then, when he was at table with them, he took the bread and blessed and broke it and gave it to them. Their eyes were opened, and they knew him; then he vanished from their sight.

They said to each other, "Did not our hearts burn within us while he talked to us on the road, while he opened to us the Scriptures?" (Luke 24:30–32). The point for us to remember—the takeaway—is that they knew him in the explication of Scripture and "the breaking of the bread."

The Book of Acts (2:42) shows us that the earliest Christians broke bread as a remembrance of the Last Supper and in anticipation of joining in the holy banquet of Lamb. By the end of the second century Scriptures were read and preached, prayers were offered, and a narration of Jesus's life flowed into the words of the Last Supper. Bread and wine were offered by invocation of the Holy Spirit upon the elements, and the people communed. This was the Lord's Supper as known among Jesus's followers after his Ascension, and it is how and why his followers still continue in "the breaking of the bread" today.

A WALK THROUGH THE SERVICE

Because the Eucharist is divided into two distinct parts (one of the Word, the other of the consecrated bread and wine at the Lord's Table), we discuss the first part of the service in this chapter, then delve into the sacramental part in the next chapter.

There are two versions of the Eucharist in the BCP 2019: the *Anglican Standard Text* (pp. 105–122) and the *Renewed Ancient Text* (pp. 123–138). We'll review both of them in the next chapter, but first, an overview of the whole service itself:

Holy Communion is normally the principal service of Christian worship on the Lord's Day, and on other appointed Feasts and Holy Days. Two forms of the liturgy, commonly called the Lord's Supper or the Holy Eucharist, are provided. The Anglican Standard Text is essentially that of the Holy Communion service of the Book of Common Prayer of 1662 and successor books through

1928, 1929, and 1962. It is presented in contemporary English and in the order for Holy Communion that is common, since the late twentieth century, among ecumenical and Anglican partners worldwide . . . The Renewed Ancient Text is drawn from liturgies of the Early Church, reflects the influence of twentieth century ecumenical consensus, and includes elements of historic Anglican piety. "Concerning the Holy Eucharist" (BCP 2019 p. 104).

The Acclamation

The celebrant (a priest or bishop who presides at the service) welcomes the assembly and says a *versicle* (a call requiring a response) from Scripture:

Celebrant: Blessed be God: the Father, the Son, and the Holy Spirit.
People: And blessed be his kingdom, now and forever.

The naming of "the Father," "the Son," and "the Holy Spirit" intentionally emphasizes the three distinct Persons of the Trinity.

The Collect for Purity

This was originally a Latin sacristy prayer to prepare the priest to say his mass, but Cranmer translated it into English so that all the assembly could prepare themselves for worship.

The Summary of the Law

Most Reformers felt that it was important to confess one's sins before meeting with God in worship. The liturgy places Jesus's Summary of the Law—to love God and one's neighbor—here or, alternatively the entire Decalogue (Ten Commandments) to re-mind people of what trespasses they might have committed.

The Kyrie

Kyrie is the Greek word for "king," which is the translation of Messiah in the Greek Old Testament, and in the very earliest liturgies that we have, even those in Latin, the Kyrie remains in Greek. At the beginning of the liturgy of the Word, a deacon led the people in a litany of intercessions that were followed by the refrain *Kyrie eleison* ("Lord, have mercy").

The Trisagion

An ancient Byzantine petition for God's mercy—"Thrice Holy"—was so named because it was usually repeated three times.

Holy God,
Holy and Mighty,
Holy Immortal One,
Have mercy upon us.

The Trisagion may be used in place of the Kyrie.

The Gloria in Excelsis

This hymn of praise recalls the Gospel of Luke's reference to the song of the angels at Jesus's birth. It is an ancient hymn or canticle that was used, especially at Christmas, from the fifth century onward. But by tradition, it should not be used during times of fasting or penitence. Therefore it is not usually sung or said during Advent or Lent.

The Collect of the Day

Collects have two functions: to transition the service from the preparatory material prior to the actual content of the Liturgy of the Word, and to focus our hearts and minds as we prepare to hear the Word. The Collect of the Day is introduced by a salutation:

Celebrant: The Lord be with you [plural].
People: And with your spirit [singular—"thy" in traditional language].

Everything done in a Eucharist is *corporate,* and this salutation links the priest and people to the action. The phrase "and with your spirit" reminds us that we worship with our whole being—body, soul, and spirit. Alternatively, congregations may respond "And also with you."

The Lessons

The purpose of the Lessons is self-evident. As stated in "A Note To The Reader," and worth repeating here, Anglicans are "a people of two books." The Bible is, according to Anglican teaching, "the word of God written" and "containing all things necessary for salvation," and is the central source of our knowledge of God and what God expects of us; and our highly participatory Prayer Book is simply "the Bible arranged for public and private worship." Selections from the Old Testament, Psalms, Epistles, and Gospels, (and on occasion the Apocrypha) are read out loud. The reading of the Gospel is the high point of the Liturgy of the Word.

Understand and remember that the Old Testament and the New Testament tell a unified story of God and his people, and that both are Holy Scripture and are bound together for this reason.

The Sermon

Preaching is essential to the Ministry of the Word in the Holy Eucharist. Based on the example of Jesus and the Apostles, clergy are commanded to "preach the word in season and out of season" (2 Timothy 4:2), and every major public service in the Prayer Book includes a sermon.

In the Middles Ages, sermons were rarely preached. Churches had no pews and the priest often mumbled the Latin (hence "hocus pocus"), so the people often fell asleep or wandered off. One of the great contributions of the Protestant Reformation was the recovery of biblical preaching. For Anglicans, the reading and the preaching of the Word are of one piece.

There are varieties of sermon types, but all must be grounded in the Scripture, usually on the Lessons of the day. Sermons should normally be full length and full strength. Shorter "homilies" may on certain occasions be appropriate, but in general the saying stands: "Sermons make Christians; sermonettes make Christianettes."

The Creeds

Three Creeds are authorized in our Prayer Book, each going more deeply into the mystery of the Trinity. They come to us for a specific purpose. Quite simply, they are Christendom's *guardrails*. The oldest and shortest is the Apostles' Creed, which emerged in the second century for use in Baptism as a confession of faith. Heresies abounded after the Church emerged from persecution, and that led to the Nicene Creed. The Council of Nicaea composed a creed in AD 325 (supplemented in 381) to overcome heresies that denied the deity of Jesus Christ. The third of the Creeds of Christendom that encapsulate the Apostolic Faith is the Creed of St. Athanasius (BCP 2019 pp. 769–771). Also called the Athanasian Creed, it isn't often used in worship services; however it is still a very valuable teaching on the Trinity and the deity of Jesus Christ.

The Prayers of the People

The Anglican Standard Text uses the *Prayer for the Whole State of Christ's Church* that first appeared in Cranmer's BCP in 1549. To make it even more participatory, it is now divided into units, each having a people's response:

> *Reader:* Lord, in your mercy:
> *People:* Hear our prayer.

It concludes with a collect said by the celebrant.

The Renewed Ancient Text, also in a litany form, serves the same ends as the Anglican Standard Text, with one significant addition, a prayer for the persecuted church.

The Confession and Absolution of Sin

The Anglican Standard Confession and Absolution is a modern translation of the 1662 rite. It begins with an invitation to pray that first appeared in Cranmer's Order for Communion of 1548.

The Comfortable Words

The "Comfortable Words" are meant to be comforting to the soul, not comfortable to the posterior in the pew. The celebrant first says, "Hear the Word of God to all who truly turn to him," followed by one or more of the four specified sentences of Scripture, e.g., "Come to me, all who labor and are heavy laden, and I will give you rest" (Matthew 11:28). The purpose is to reassure the people that Jesus Christ is *welcoming* and that he is their source of comfort in this world.

Archbishop Cranmer intended these four Scriptural verses as a summary of all the "good news" of the Gospel.

The Peace

The BCP 2019 rubric reads, "Then the Ministers and People may greet one another in the Name of the Lord."

Based on St. Paul's frequent commendation to "Greet each other with a holy kiss,"—think the manner of many Europeans at a family affair—members of the congregation greet each other with an embrace, a handshake or simply a smile. The Peace is intended to be solemn though it may be hearty, reminding us of Jesus' words at the Last Supper: "Peace I leave with you; my peace I give to you. Not as the world gives do I give to you" (John 14:27).

This ends our discussion of the LITURGY OF THE WORD. In the next chapter, we take up the second part of the Eucharistic service —THE LITURGY OF THE TABLE OR SERVICE OF COMMUNION.

Chapter 7

The Holy Eucharist:
The Liturgy of the Table

(BCP 2019 pp. 114–122 or 131–138)

PURPOSE

The action and focus of the liturgy now moves from the lectern and pulpit to the Lord's Table, also known as the Altar.

A WALK THROUGH THE LITURGY OF THE TABLE

The purpose of the Eucharist is to encounter Jesus in the breaking of the bread in the context of a meal that represents our personal participation in his Last Supper and our anticipation of the Heavenly Banquet. The BCP 2019 offers us two distinct but equally valuable texts for this liturgy: the Anglican Standard Text and the Renewed Ancient Text. The Anglican Standard Text is closer to the Prayer Book of the English Reformation, while the Renewed Ancient Text reflects the modern recovery of an ancient liturgy from the 3rd or 4th century attributed to St.

Hippolytus of Rome. Many contemporary liturgies reflect this pattern of celebrating the Eucharist.

The order of the parts in the Anglican Standard Text and the Renewed Ancient Text is the same, as are the common texts for the congregational response: the Offertory, the Sursum Corda, the Sanctus, the Lord's Prayer, the Fraction, the Prayer of Humble Access, the Agnus Dei, the Ministration of Communion, the Post Communion Prayer (the one exception, with different wording), the Blessing, and the Dismissal. The Prayers of Consecration, however, show differences, which we shall examine below.

The Offertory

The entire Liturgy of the Table may be seen as an offering, of God's gift to us of salvation in Christ and our grateful reception of that gift. In the words of the classic Prayer Book: "Here we offer and present to you, O Lord, ourselves, our souls and bodies, to be a reasonable, holy and living sacrifice. . . . And although we are unworthy because of our many sins to offer you any sacrifice, yet we ask you to accept this our bounden duty and service." These balanced phrases, a hallmark of the Protestant Reformation, recognize that we have nothing to give God that he needs and that the only thing God desires of us is our gratitude and our love.

From the list on BCP 2019 pp. 149–151, the celebrant chooses one or more sentences of Scripture to read to the assembly. It is a sign that preparations at the Holy Table are beginning to be made for the consecration. A psalm or hymn "covers" the movements of the ushers and clergy as offerings are brought forward. As the offerings are presented, Scripture from 1 Chronicles 29:11, 14 may be recited, which captures the twofold nature of the offering: "All things come from you, O Lord, *And of your own have we given you.*"

The Sursum Corda

The Sursum Corda exhorts the people to enthusiastic and participatory worship. It begins with a salutation ("The Lord be with you") to stress the importance of lifting our hearts heavenward in praise. The calls and responses create a dialogue that focuses on praise. It is found in all the earliest manuscripts, and certainly was already in common use in the second century.

The Sanctus

The Sanctus uses an ecumenical translation of a text that originated in the fourth century. The Sanctus takes its name from Isaiah's vision of God in the Temple—"Holy, holy, holy is the Lord of Hosts"—and concludes with Jesus's entry into Jerusalem where the crowds cried: "Blessed is he who comes in the Name of the Lord. Hosanna in the highest."

The Prayer of Consecration

In some church traditions, the Prayer of Consecration involves a mere recitation of Jesus's Words of Institution at the Last Supper ("This is my body. . . . This is my blood"). This not the case with either the Anglican Standard Text or the Renewed Ancient Text. In both, the Prayer of Consecration is lengthy, and at this point you should take time to read the two versions of the text (BCP pp. 115–117 and 132–134).

Both texts are extended prayers to God the Father. Both texts include two key moments—or movements, as in a symphony—the *anamnesis*, "recounting" the mighty acts of God, and the *epiclesis*, "invoking" the Spirit's presence. The focus in the *anamnesis* in the Anglican Standard Text is on Jesus's "full, perfect, and sufficient sacrifice, oblation, and satisfaction for the sins of the whole world." Likewise its *epiclesis*, which comes before the Words of Institution, asks the Father "to bless and sanctify with your Word and Holy Spirit these gifts of bread and wine, that we, receiving them according to your Son our Savior Jesus Christ's holy institution, in remembrance of his death and passion, may be partakers of his most blessed Body and Blood." The dynamic interaction of the Word, the Spirit, and the believer is character-istic of Anglican liturgy.

In the Renewed Ancient Text, the *anamnesis* begins by recall-ing the action of the loving Father, "who made us for yourself" and who, "when we had sinned against you and become subject to evil and death," sent his Son, who took on our flesh "by the Holy Spirit and the Virgin Mary," who "stretched out his arms on the Cross and offered himself once for all," and who rose from the dead and "broke the bonds of death, trampling Hell and Sa-tan under his feet." In this text, the Words of Institution appear at the climax of the divine action, the Passion of Jesus Christ, summed up in the acclamation: "Christ has died, Christ is risen, Christ will come again." The twofold *epiclesis* then consummates the action: "Sanctify [the gifts of Bread and Wine] by your Word and Holy Spirit to be for your people the Body and Blood of your Son Jesus Christ. Sanctify us also that we may worthily receive this holy Sacrament, and be made one body with him, that he may dwell in us and we in him."

Both texts conclude with praise of the Triune God, followed by a strong Amen from the congregation.

The Lord's Prayer

The Lord's Prayer follows the Prayer of Consecration and leads to the "breaking of the bread" in most modern ecumenical rites. There are two versions of the Lord's Prayer, stemming from lit-tle differences found in the sources (Matthew 6:9–13 and Luke

11:1–4). However, the essentials are the same and are the pattern for Christian prayer: (1) We bless God and pray for our world, our communities, and our lives to be shaped by his will; (2) we pray for our daily needs to be met; (3) we pray for forgiveness for wrongs that we and others have committed, and (4) we pray for strength to resist temptation and for protection from danger. Ancient sources added a doxology at the end: "For yours is the kingdom . . ."

The Fraction

In early Western rites, the breaking of loaves of bread and the pouring and mixing of large quantities of wine could take quite some time, so the *Agnus Dei* was placed here to cover the actions taking place at the Holy Table. The Fraction as a title is not a part of the 1662 or 1928 Prayer Book tradition, in which the priest broke the bread at the Words of Institution. The BCP 2019 provides the option of breaking the bread after the Lord's Prayer with reference by St. Paul to "Christ our Passover . . . is sacrificed for us" (1 Corinthians 5:7). The alternative wording "is sacrificed, once for all upon the Cross" makes clear the unique sacrifice of Jesus "once for all" (Hebrews 7:27).

The Prayer of Humble Access

Cranmer composed the Prayer of Humble Access, and it has become one of the most memorable prayers in the English language, reflecting the attitude of the publican in Jesus' parable: "God, be merciful on me, a sinner" (Luke 18:13). He considered the prayer a necessity for the people, since the old custom of infrequent communion, and the fear of condemnation if one was not worthy to receive kept many from having frequent communion. So the celebrant and the people say, "We do not presume to come to this your table, O merciful Lord, trusting in our own righteousness . . ."

The Agnus Dei

The Agnus Dei ("Lamb of God") is both scriptural (John 1:19) and ancient (fourth century). It appears in BCP 2019 to remind us of Jesus's sacrifice of himself for our benefit.

The Ministration of Communion

The breaking of the bread, as at the Last Supper of Jesus and his disciples, lends the imagery of a "feeding" of guests, as at a banquet. Also recall that when one of the soldiers pierced Jesus's side with his spear "at once there came out blood and water" (John 19:34). And so the wine, representing Jesus's blood, will be mixed with water. It is yet another evidence of Jesus being both divine and human.

Before administering the sacrament, the celebrant may invite worshipers to the Lord's Table with one of these words:

The gifts of God for the people of God. Take them in remembrance that Christ died for you and feed on him in your hearts by faith, with thanksgiving.

Or

Behold the Lamb of God, behold him who takes away the sins of the world. Blessed are those who are invited to the marriage supper of the Lamb.

There are many different ways Anglicans share in the Holy Communion. The rubric suggests that "hymns, songs, or anthems may be sung." Usually communicants receive the sacrament with a personal time of silent reverence.

The Post Communion Prayer

This prayer is a modern version of the original Cranmer prayer. In his time, the priest alone said a private prayer at this point, but Cranmer felt that it was pastorally important to have a common prayer of thanksgiving said by all who had communed.

The Blessing

Cranmer put this great prayer together from a combination of quotations in Philippians 4:7 and Numbers 6:24–28, together with Trinitarian names. "The peace of God, which passeth all understanding, keep your hearts and minds in the knowledge and love of God . . ."

The Dismissal

The Dismissal was not a part of any of the of the historic Anglican Prayer Books. A dismissal is ancient however, and appears in the earliest service books of the Western Church. BCP 2019 pp. 122 and 138 offer four choices, such as, "Go in peace to love and serve the Lord." From the Easter Vigil through the Day of Pentecost, "Alleluia, alleluia" is added to any of the dismissals. It may be added at other times, except during Lent and on other penitential occasions.

APPLICATION

Prayer Book tradition has always included a conscious preparation before one comes forward to the altar rail for Communion. The expectation had been that one had fasted before receiving Communion—or at least had spent time reflecting on any misconduct or sin that should be confessed, as all recite the Confession and receive Absolution.

The words of the Communion liturgy should be our guide in realizing that at each Communion we are physically and spiritually linked with "angels and archangels, and all the company of Heaven," and most of all that we are joined with the presence of our Lord, who is here to invite us into his life and his love! Once we leave the altar rail we should understand that we are now a "Christ-bearer," and that as we depart the church building, we are carrying Christ out into the world of our daily living.

Part Two

The Church: Rites and Resources

Chapter 8

Holy Baptism

(BCP 2019 pp. 161–173)

PURPOSE

The two Sacraments ordained by Jesus Christ himself are Holy Communion and Holy Baptism. Baptism in water in the name of the Father, and of the Son, and of the Holy Spirit is the unchanging core of the Church's initiatory sacrament.

Unlike the Eucharist, which is celebrated Sunday by Sunday among Anglicans, Baptism is done only once, because it is the once for all mark of a once for all salvation. It is the entrance of the baptized person into the Body of Christ as a full member of the family of the faithful. Importantly, one is not baptized into one denomination or another but into Christ's Church, "the whole company of all faithful people."

In Matthew 28:18–20, Jesus commanded us to baptize. The act of Baptism is one's participation in Christ's death and in his resurrection. It brings about a new life in Christ that washes away sin and gives new birth, enlightenment, renewal by the Holy Spirit, and the promise of eternal life.

CHARACTERISTICS

The Sacrament of Baptism is the beginning of a Christian's journey toward the stature of the fullness of Christ which has been promised to all who believe in him (Ephesians 4:13). It is the "outward and visible sign of an inward and spiritual grace." The actions of Baptism in the 1549 through 1662 Prayer Books included the option of being immersed in water and signed with a cross on one's forehead, with the words, "I baptize you in the name of the Father, and the Son, and the Holy Ghost."

Immersion remains a common method of baptism, but virtually all early representations (mosaics) of baptism show the method as pouring water over the head. This latter means will be found in the majority of Anglican baptisms today.

Baptism is meant to be a "public" event that takes place in the midst of the congregation. The order of a Baptism service comprises these parts: the Presentation of Candidates, their Profession of Faith, their Baptism in water, their signing with the cross, and the celebration of Holy Communion.

BACKGROUND

The earliest Baptismal Rite we know of comes from the late third century, but references to rites of Baptism exist from much earlier times. Baptism was then a long and involved preparation—as much as forty days of catechizing, fasting and prayer.

However, at the time of the Reformation, there was a wide divergence about the number of sacraments and the meaning of Baptism and how it was practiced. Lutherans and Anglicans accepted the traditional definition of the sacrament as "an outward and visible sign of an inward and spiritual grace," but added that there had to be a biblical record of Jesus's own institution of the sacrament, and only Baptism and the Lord's Supper satisfied that requirement. Other Christians, such as Baptists, saw baptism as not an act of God but an act of the believer to demonstrate their conversion.

Baptism was centered on infants as a long and stable practice. The New Testament (Acts 16:15,33; 18:8; 1 Corinthians 1:16) records whole households being baptized. Yet infant baptism became increasingly complicated as the twentieth century moved forward. Baptism as a mere sign of family identity or cultural membership—"getting the child done" in a private service—took away any sense of divine action. Thus the BCP 2019 renewed, rather than revolutionized, the Prayer Book tradition for the Sacrament of Baptism.

A WALK THROUGH THE BAPTISMAL RITES

The Introduction

The Introduction begins with the ancient definition of a sacrament as the reason for Baptism. It follows the same reasons that Cranmer first gave in the 1549 BCP for a public Baptism in church—that it should be administered along with the Eucharist on Sundays or Holy Days, so that the congregation may be edified by it.

Each of the candidates should have sponsors "who themselves are committed to Christ and have been commended by their example of their own holy living." If the candidates are not old enough to speak for themselves, the sponsors who present them then make promises in their own names, as well as vows on behalf of their candidates. Adult candidates and the sponsors and parents of children should have been instructed in the meaning of Baptism and in their particular duties, so they can help the new Christians grow in the knowledge and love of God.

The Exhortation

The Exhortation lays out the very reasons for Baptism: our need for forgiveness of sins, Jesus's command that all who believe in him should be baptized, our death to our old life and our rebirth to new life in Christ, and the bestowal of the Holy Spirit. The candidates are then presented.

The Vows or Promises

The vows or promises made by the sponsors of infants are significant. They are asked if they can make these vows for themselves, and if they will promise to fulfill their role as sponsors by making sure that the child is taught the meaning of these vows and of the faith as revealed in Scripture. They also agree to ensure the child will learn the basics of the Faith—the Creeds, the Lord's Prayer, and the Ten Commandments—so that they shall "come to put their faith in Jesus Christ," stressing an experience of faith, rather than just knowledge of faith.

Renunciations and Affirmations

Next are the ancient renunciations and affirmations that are found in the earliest baptismal texts. By saying forcefully "I renounce them"—referring to the world, the flesh and the devil—the candidates acknowledge the reality of evil. Then saying equally forcefully "I do," and "I will," they commit themselves to Jesus Christ, to the Bible and the Creeds, and to a life of obedience.

Litany and Prayers

A short litany follows that is focused on the candidates and concludes with Cranmer's adaptation of Luther's "Flood Prayer," a reference to God's salvation via the Ark through water.

Thanksgiving Over the Water

When the celebrant and candidates process to the font, the celebrant blesses the water in an *epiclesis,* an invocation of the Holy Spirit, that parallels the Sursum Corda at the Eucharist. The celebrant touches the water and asks the Father to send down the Holy Spirit upon the font and on the candidates. Just before the actual Baptism, the celebrant may ask the parents or sponsors to "Name this child," which reminds all present that each child has a personal identity before God and a particular human family, just as the baby Jesus was named at his circumcision (Luke 2:21).

The Baptism

The actual Baptism itself may be performed either by immersion or infusion. *Immersion* can happen in a wide variety of ways and contexts, inside or outside the church building. *Infusion* means pouring water on or over the person to be baptized. Most ancient depictions of Baptism show the individuals kneeling in water up to their chest and large amounts of water poured over their heads and shoulders. Mere sprinkling isn't recommended because it doesn't have any visible relationship to drowning the old in order to bring on the new.

Sign of the Cross and Anointing

Once the Baptism is performed and the candidate is clothed and dry, the celebrant makes the sign of the cross on the baptized person's forehead with water or sacred oil. The anointing should be much more than a mere thumb on the head; it should be a generous amount that suggests being soaked in the Holy Spirit.

Giving of a White Garment and Candle

Two ancient customs have been restored as options to the post-baptismal rites: the giving of a white garment to the newly baptized to represent their righteousness after the washing away of their sin, and the giving of a candle to represent the Light of Christ.

Prayer, Welcome of the Newly Baptized, and the Peace

The celebrant prays a prayer derived from the 1662 rite and then asks the assembly to welcome the newly baptized. The Peace concludes the Baptism and acts as the transition into the Eucharist that follows.

APPLICATION

Baptism is indelible and unrepeatable and marks one a child of God forever. But that does not mean that Baptism is a magic shield that will resist the assaults of the devil or one's straying from God's pathways. As St. Paul remarks in Romans 3:23, "All have sinned and fall short of the glory of God," and we all do so daily. Our own baptism should come to mind frequently, reminding us of who exactly we are in Christ. Martin Luther, when under spiritual attack by the devil, would shout "*I am Baptized,*" and even threw inkpots against the wall for emphasis!

Luther also famously described himself as *simul justus et peccator*—a justified sinner. To be a saint is to be someone through whom God's love and light shines. To be a saint (that is, to be a "holy person") is not something that we can accomplish by ourselves. We all ought to renew our baptismal vows every day of our lives, and when we fall short, we should ask God to forgive us and send the Spirit to renew us in our commitment. But how do we do this?

A simple way is every morning when you wake up, mark your forehead with the sign of the Cross, remember your baptismal vows, and ask for God's help to keep them that day and day by day. Then at bedtime reflect on the events of your day to consider the ways in which God drew near to you and the ways you fell short of God's call on your life. Ask God for forgiveness and the grace to do better tomorrow. The Collect for Grace memorized is a good way to do this.

Many churches have a baptismal font at the church entrance, so that the people who enter can dip their fingers in the water and remember their Baptism. This was an ancient Christian custom, when people always washed their feet, hands, and faces before they prayed, whether at their church or in their homes.

Can you not think of some actions that might encourage you to renew your Baptism, day by day?

Chapter 9

Confirmation

(BCP 2019 pp. 174–193)

PURPOSE

Confirmation is not a sacrament ordained by Christ as necessary for salvation. Rather, it arises from the practice of the Apostles and of the Early Church. One reason for the rite of Confirmation is so that those who were baptized as infants may, as they mature in their faith, have a way of demonstrating that they are fulfilling the vows made for them at their Baptism. In the popular mind, Confirmation may simply be a rite of joining a local church. But it is much deeper than that. The bishop's participation shows that it is both an affirmation of the believer and a rite of passage whereby one is commissioned to pray and work for the worldwide spread of the Gospel (Matthew 28:18–20). It is a personal recommitting to Christ and a public agreeing to be in fellowship and ministry with the whole Church throughout the world.

CHARACTERISTICS

It is clear from the beginning that two things were essential to the rite: the presence of a bishop who could lay his hands upon those who were baptized, and an adult confession of faith. Confirmation serves as a rite to reaffirm baptismal vows at various stages of a Christian's pilgrimage, combining knowledge of the faith from the Catechism with a mentoring of the believer for the actual practice of it.

BACKGROUND

The practice of Confirmation in the early Church was that a candidate was baptized in water by a deacon or priest and then anointed with chrism by the bishop as a sign of receiving the gifts of the Holy Spirit. This was done at one service, usually at Epiphany, the Easter Vigil, or Pentecost. The earliest baptismal ceremonies involved relatively small, tight-knit communities of believers who were faced with persecution. Local families often waited until the bishop could come to lay hands on the newly baptized and anoint them with chrism to invoke the Holy Spirit.

Later the preparation required for Confirmation became all too often a mere memorization of doctrine rather than the mentoring of a disciple into a mature and personal faith. This question remains today: How does a faith community bring baptized but "unformed" infants into a mature faith as adults?

A "baptismal revolution" in the 1970s rightly thought that Confirmation seen as a "rite of passage" into adulthood was inadequate and archaic. The ACNA College of Bishops deliberated about the purpose of Confirmation and decided that it was not the "completion" of Baptism, but a self-standing and repeatable rite on its own. Its purpose was to provide a "public and personal profession of faith from every adult believer in Jesus

Christ." They justified the need for such a rite by referring to the Scriptures, especially 2 Timothy 1:6–7 and Acts 8:14–17, which record the Apostles laying their hands on those who had been baptized. They also saw a pastoral need to extend the laying on of hands beyond confirmation to the "reception" of adults from other Christian traditions, and for those who were returning to the faith or being renewed in the Spirit and wished to publicly reaffirm their baptismal vows.

Since the bishop is the overseer of the diocese and represents the wider Church, it is appropriate that the bishop be the one to lay hands on and pray for those who wish to affirm or reaffirm their faith in the one holy catholic and apostolic Church.

A WALK THROUGH CONFIRMATION

The service may be a stand-alone event or it may be combined with Morning Prayer or Evening Prayer, but the preferred way is to include it in a Eucharist service. The visitation of the bishop to a local congregation is a most appropriate time for the bishop to exercise his pastoral care in both baptizing and confirming.

The service begins with a greeting, either the one specifically for initiation rites or a seasonal one. The bishop prays the Collect of the Day and uses the lessons for the day or lessons especially appropriate to Baptism or Confirmation. A sermon is preached often with an exhortation to the confirmands, followed by the Nicene Creed.

The candidates are then presented to the bishop. He introduces the reasons for this rite and asks the candidates to renew their baptismal vows. The assembly is then asked if they will support the candidates in their Christian life. The bishop prays over the candidates and lays hands on each candidate individually. A final prayer is prayed, and if there is no Eucharist, the Lord's Prayer is added before the blessing.

APPLICATION

Do you remember your own Baptism? Most Anglicans who grew up in the Church would not remember their Baptism as infants. We believe that Baptism is what we receive from God, not what we do; the term *"prevenient grace"* means that God, through the Holy Spirit, calls us into relationship with himself even before we consciously realize his call on our life. When we seek to be confirmed, we are responding to the call God made to us at our Baptism, in recognition that the seed that was planted in us at our Baptism has grown into a mature relationship that we now ask God to deepen within us.

Even as we "remember" our Baptism when we participate in the Baptism of others, we should also "remember" our own confirmation when we attend a service of Confirmation. God "saved us" at our Baptism (1 Peter 3:21), and we respond to God's call at our Confirmation.

It is never too often to give God thanks for his prevenient grace in our lives!

Chapter 10

Pastoral Rites

(BCP 2019 pp. 198–266)

Six Pastoral Rites

HOLY MATRIMONY—THANKSGIVING FOR THE BIRTH OR
ADOPTION OF A CHILD—RITES OF HEALING—MINISTRY TO
THE DYING—PRAYERS FOR A VIGIL—BURIAL OF THE DEAD

A pastoral rite is a formal text and liturgy relating to particular occasions and stages of life from birth to death. The Prayer Book offers particular ritual forms for these occasions.

Holy Matrimony

(BCP 2019 pp. 198–214)

Marriage is as old as human history. Nearly all societies require a marriage contract to ensure property and inheritance within a family, and certainly stable families are an absolutely necessary building block for societal cohesion. Christians see matrimony as a sacred estate instituted by God at creation and blessed by him. What God intended in the estate of marriage can be expressed using two words: covenant and sacrament.

For Christians, a covenant relationship of husband and wife is not just a covenant between them, but it is also a covenant they make with God. This is why the Prayer Book speaks of "holy" matrimony. Whether marriage is described as covenant and sacrament, it remains a supernatural relationship that should be supported by the Church, the community of faith.

While the doctrine of marriage is derived from the Old Testament and the teaching of Jesus, the marriage rite was clearly defined by the second century. As early as the eighth century the basic shape and content of the rite has remained constant. Conservative Reformers such as Luther and Cranmer saw marriage as a sacred vocation to be conducted by a minister in the context of a church service and to include a nuptial blessing. Thomas Cranmer established marriage as a religious ceremony to be performed in the church, with a fixed ritual order.

BCP 2019 has this to say about Holy Matrimony:

In Holy Matrimony, God establishes and blesses the covenant between husband and wife, and joins them to live together in a communion of love, faithfulness, and peace within the fellowship of Christ and His Church. God enables all married people to grow in love, wisdom, and godliness through a common life patterned on the sacrificial love of Christ. (p. 198)

The Introduction to marriage opens with the famous words of the classic Book of Common Prayer:

Dearly beloved: We have gathered together in the presence of God to witness and bless the joining together of this man and this woman in Holy Matrimony.

Almighty God established the bond and covenant of marriage in creation as a sign of the mystical union between Christ and his Church. Our Lord Jesus Christ adorned this manner of life by his presence and first miracle at a wedding in Cana of Galilee, and it is commended by Holy Scripture to be held in honor among all people.

The liturgy then proceeds to give four purposes for Holy Matrimony: the procreation of children; the mutual love, help and society of husband and wife; the maintenance of sexual purity; and the upbuilding of society.

This introduction is followed by the "betrothal vows," which completes the couple's preparations for marriage which had been announced in a series of "banns" and by signing a "Declaration of Intention." Then follow a set of lessons and a sermon. The sermon is an ideal opportunity for the priest to reach the many outsiders who are in attendance with the Gospel.

Finally, the couple takes their solemn vows before God "to have and to hold [one another] from this day forward, for better for worse, for richer for poorer, in sickness and in health, to love and cherish until we are parted by death." After the exchange of rings, the service continues with prayers and the nuptial blessing by the priest or bishop in the name of the Trinity.

Frequently, this beautiful and significant ceremony concludes with the Holy Communion.

The Anglican Church in North America maintains a high standard of marital fidelity. Many of the details of the marriage are governed by national or diocesan canons, including on rare occasion and only on New Testament grounds the possibility of remarriage after divorce.

Thanksgiving for the Birth or Adoption of a Child

(BCP 2019 pp. 215–221)
The birth or adoption of a child is always an occasion for thanksgiving and prayer in family and community. Two opening

addresses are provided, one for a birth and the other for an adoption. This rite is provided for use in a hospital or home, during public worship, or in some other appropriate place.

The *Magnificat* or Psalm 116 is said by all, and if the rite is not in public worship, it continues with the Kyrie and the Lord's Prayer. Prayers follow for the child, parents, siblings, and birth parents of an adopted child. This rite does not replace Baptism. The parents are encouraged not to defer baptism of the child. This rite can be used even if the mother or child dies in childbirth (BCP 2019 p. 215).

In the present day, infertility troubles affect many couples; also the loss of a child in pregnancy can cause severe depression in the hopeful mother. However, the rite does not deal with such issues directly. Ministering to such couples must be handled with grace and delicacy.

Rites of Reconciliation and Healing

Reconciliation and healing are intimately connected ministries of Jesus and the Church. Pastors are called to heal the sick, to comfort the afflicted, and to prepare individuals and their family for death. The Prayer Book contains helpful rites for all these situations.

Reconciliation of Penitents

(BCP 2019 pp. 223–224)
To be human is to sin against God, against our neighbor—and even against ourselves. The burden of knowing that we have "fallen short" is hard to bear. Yet sadly, so many of us avoid facing the unpleasant, and particularly the unacceptable. Scripture is very clear that we can confess our sins directly to God, and if we are truly penitent, God will forgive us. Thus to know who we

really are, and *whose* we really are, we need to see ourselves as God sees us, and forgive as God forgives us.

It is relatively easy to tell God that we are sorry when we pray alone, but it is a different experience when we have to say things for which we are ashamed aloud to another person. But the purpose of confession is not to burden us with guilt; it is just the opposite—to receive the grace of being *reconciled* to God, our neighbor and, yes, ourselves. When we sin we must not run *from* Jesus, we must run *to* him.

Unlike the sacraments of Holy Communion or Baptism, the Rite of Reconciliation has no external "signs." If someone feels burdened in conscience or is haunted by past offences that just won't go away, it can be extremely helpful for that person to meet with a priest who can act as God's representative. Whatever is said or confessed to the confessor is forgotten as soon as the penitent is forgiven. A confessor is under the strict "seal of the confessional" and cannot tell anyone what was said. And at the end of the rite the priest says, "Go in peace and pray for me, a sinner"—an appropriate endnote that reminds us that we all have fallen short of the glory of God.

Nonetheless, always remember that anyone can ask God directly for forgiveness, without any need for a mediator or go-between, but the go-between often proves of immense help in letting go of the shame and guilt associated with sin. One helpful rule in deciding whether to go to a confessor is: "Some may, none must, some should."

Ministry to the Sick

(BCP 2019 pp. 225–235)
Humans are not just body and mind. We were created by the Triune God to be of a triune nature ourselves. We are body, soul, and spirit, which are meant to be in equilibrium. If one

side of the triangle is off balance, the whole system becomes diseased.

Jesus preached the message of God's reign to exemplify what the fullness of life is meant to be, and healing was central to his ministry. His disciples continued that ministry by spoken prayer, laying on of hands and anointing with oil (James 5:14); and the ministry is also ours as members of Christ's body, the Church.

The Rites of Healing are not meant to be in competition with the healing practices of the modern world. God uses the gifts of researchers, physicians, and psychological counselors to heal us as well.

Jesus recognized that illness was spiritual as well as physical, and he instructed his disciples to offer a ministry of reconciliation and absolution to those troubled by broken relationships and broken promises. Because physical, emotional, and spiritual healing are often interrelated, it is particularly appropriate to encourage confession, reconciliation, and forgiveness in the context of ministry to the sick.

The Healing Rites continue from BCP 2019 pp. 225–235 and include services of Ministry to the Sick, and Communion of the Sick, along with appropriate prayers and Scripture passages.

Ministry to the Dying

(BCP 2019 pp. 236–242)
Death is the last great mystery facing us as human beings. What happens after we die? Various religions suggest answers such as reincarnation or some sort of bodiless existence beyond physical death, and others offer no hope of ongoing survival at all. Christianity is the faith whose founder is "the resurrection and the life." Those who receive him are promised eternal life with him.

In his book, *Our Greatest Gift: A Meditation on Dying and Caring,* Henri Nouwen tells a parable of faith and hope. He imagines twins, a brother and a sister, talking to each other in their mother's womb:

> The sister said to the brother, "I believe there is life after birth." Her brother protested vehemently, "No, no, this is all there is. This is a dark and cozy place, and we have nothing else to do but to cling to the cord that feeds us." The little girl insisted, "There must be something more than this dark place. There must be something else, a place with light where there is freedom to move." Still, she could not convince her twin brother.
>
> After some silence, the sister said hesitantly, "I have something else to say, and I'm afraid you won't believe that, either, but I think there is a mother." Her brother became furious. "A mother!" he shouted. "What are you talking about? I have never seen a mother, and neither have you. Who put that idea in your head? As I told you, this place is all we have. Why do you always want more? This is not such a bad place, after all. We have all we need, so let's be content."
>
> The sister was quite overwhelmed by her brother's response and for a while didn't dare say anything more. But she couldn't let go of her thoughts, and since she had only her twin brother to speak to, she finally said, "Don't you feel these squeezes every once in a while? They're quite unpleasant and sometimes even painful." "Yes," he answered. "What's special about that?" "Well," the sister said, "I think that these squeezes are there to get us ready for another place, much more beautiful than this, where we will see our mother face-to-face. Don't you think that's exciting?"
>
> The brother didn't answer. He was fed up with the foolish talk of his sister and felt that the best thing would be simply to ignore her and hope that she would leave him alone.

We can live as if this life were all we had, as if death were absurd and we had better not talk about it; or we can choose to claim our divine inheritance and trust that death is the painful but blessed passage that will bring us face-to-face with our God. Ministry to the dying provides the opportunity to speak honestly with the patient and family about what counts most in life and whether they are prepared to settle their accounts with each other and with God. And yes, it is evangelism too for those in attendance who have not received the Lord.

A WALK THROUGH THE TEXTS

The BCP 2019 "Ministry to the Dying" includes three distinct services. The first helps a dying person prepare for death with loved ones gathered around. The second is a short vigil service to be used at the funeral home or church before the actual funeral. Burial of the Dead is the third service. The whole focus of the burial is intended to evoke the "Paschal Mystery" of Christ's death and resurrection, and the Christian hope of being ourselves resurrected to meet our Lord face-to-face. Each step on this pilgrimage is meant to bring the reality of death into the joy of the resurrection. The rubric on p. 236 says, "When a person is near death, the minister should be notified." This is an important consideration, for it is very helpful to the family that the minister be involved in the entire progression from sickness to death.

THE LITANY AT THE TIME OF DEATH (BCP P. 237) is an ancient prayer that was written in the eighth century. It can be said responsively with the family and allows them to actively participate in the transition that will take place. At the final hour, a Prayer of Commendation is said by the leader, and those assembled may recite together the *Nunc Dimittis*, "Lord, now let your servant depart in peace . . ." (BCP p. 241)

A VIGIL can be led by anyone, but it is appropriate that if the minister is present, he should preside. The vigil may include Psalm 23 and/or 121 and a Scripture reading. Two prayers may be read: one for the person who has died and the other for their family. The prayers conclude with the Lord's Prayer and a concluding blessing. The Vigil can be repeated if there are long visiting hours or some days before the funeral.

The Burial of the Dead

(BCP pp. 248–266)
The funeral rite is designed for use in a church and presumes that the deceased is a baptized and practicing Christian. Not infrequently, clergy will agree to preside at a funeral home and speak charitably of the deceased. In such situations it is important to include in the message the truth that Jesus is the way, the truth, and the life and that "if Christ has not been raised, then our preaching is in vain and your faith is in vain" (1 Corinthians 15:14).

A Christian funeral is an act of faith and a witness to the world. Along with weddings, a funeral is one of the few places where non-believers mingle and encounter the Easter Gospel enacted in a public liturgy. The Introduction stresses that the service looks forward to eternal life and not backward to past events. It is no occasion for eulogies or family remembrances (which are better placed at the Vigil or a Reception following the service). The readings and music should all be biblical and dignified, as befits the solemn occasion.

The one presiding meets the body at the door and proceeds before it to the chancel. In the Anglican tradition, the coffin is closed and covered with a pall. The Collect, readings, and a homily follow. If the service is not to have Holy Communion, the Apostles' Creed and Lord's Prayer are said.

If there is Holy Communion, the liturgy continues with the Prayers and moves into the Eucharist. A Proper Preface and a Post-Communion Prayer is provided. The one presiding moves to the head of the coffin during a short Litany and concludes with a commending prayer. The body is borne out of the church.

THE COMMITTAL is to be performed at the burial site. It assumes a grave but may be a mausoleum or some other place of rest. If the body was cremated, the ashes should also be buried in the ground or set in a columbarium. Christians believe in the resurrection of the body and the integral relationship of the body with a spiritual soul. Burial of the body or the ashes is an important symbol of that unity that is to be continued after death.

APPLICATION

What should we do now to prepare for our own death? It is a great benefit to our families for us to prepare a will that includes references to where we would have the funeral and where we would be buried. We should also give the parish priest a list of directions regarding our funeral, rather than leaving our loved ones to make these decisions after we're gone. Many parishes have a form that can be filled out to select appropriate Scripture readings, hymns, music, etc. The parish priest should be notified of a death at the same time the funeral director is notified, so that he can be with the family as things proceed.

Chapter 11

The Psalter

(BCP 2019 pp. 269–467)

PURPOSE

Psalms are poetry rather than prose. They are meant to be said or sung out loud or in quiet meditation. They are inspirational, not informational. They are also *multivalent,* which means they have multiple layers of meaning that can spark our imagination. As we recite them, the words and images become *memorable*; they should sink deeply into our hearts so that God can then use words and images to communicate with us.

In the Bible, the Psalms are the 150 prayers and praises attributed to the shepherd boy who became the king of Israel around 1000 BC. We find the story of David singing as he played his harp before King Saul in 1 Samuel 16:16–19.

But how can poetry, some of which is 3,000 years old, have any relevance in modern society? For at least three solid reasons, we should engage with the Psalms, both in public worship and especially in our private devotions: *God has not changed, we have not changed, and our range of emotions has not changed.* We still experience joy and sorrow, fear and hatred; and we still need to bare our souls before God.

CHARACTERISTICS

The Psalms were the chief prayer book of Jesus. Jesus often quoted from the Psalms, which he did even as he was hanging on the cross, "My God, my God, why have you forsaken me?" (Psalm 22). The Gospel writers often related quotations from the Psalms to events in Jesus's own life and ministry. The New Testament quotes from the Psalms more than ninety times.

The Psalms have been and still are a major source of dialogue between God and his people. The Church has long seen Christ's presence in the Psalms, either as words spoken *about* him or describing him, or as words coming *from* him as the Messiah, the son of David. You will recognize Jesus in Psalms 1, 2, 18, 20, 21, 45, 110, and 118.

BACKGROUND

The Psalms had long been used for worship in the Jerusalem temple. After its destruction by the Babylonians around 587 BC, the Psalms became the prayerful songs of the Jews who had been scattered from their homeland (Psalm 137). The Jewish people continue to chant the Psalms wherever the are.

In public worship, the Psalms are either said in unison by the congregation or recited, sung or chanted "responsively" or "antiphonally," meaning that each verse is divided into two parts having a common theme. In the synagogues in Jesus's time, singing probably alternated by half-verse, much as Anglicans traditionally recite or sing responsively.

The BCP 2019 has included a "revised Coverdale translation" of the Psalter. In so doing it is restoring a gem of the original English Prayer Books. The translation by Miles Coverdale in 1535 predated the King James Bible and it remained the standard because the Coverdale Psalter had become so well known to the English people. That Psalter remained the standard for all later Prayer Books up to and including the 1928 American BCP.

In 1963 a group of English scholars, which included C. S. Lewis and T. S. Eliot, produced an updated version of the Coverdale Psalter. ACNA Archbishop Duncan, who had learned the Coverdale Psalter by heart, suggested to the scholars working on an ACNA Psalter translation that they should revisit the 1963 translation, both for its memorable phrases and its poetic flow. The result is the NEW COVERDALE PSALTER found in the Book of Common Prayer 2019. The NEW COVERDALE PSALTER is also available separately in a fine NEW COVERDALE PSALTER leather-bound edition.

A WALK THROUGH THE PSALTER

The organization of the New Coverdale Psalter respectfully maintains its historic roots. The Psalm numbers follow the original division of the Hebrew text into five books comprising the 150 Psalms. From the fourth century onward, it became the custom to end each Psalm with a Christian doxology ("Glory be to the Father, and to the Son, and to the Holy Spirit . . ."). The doxology can be used after each set of Psalms, or after each individual Psalm. This custom emphasizes the continuity between the Old and the New Testaments, being a unified story of God and his people. And as Holy Spirit-inspired Scripture, the Psalms remain for us the voice of our Lord speaking to us.

The preface to the Psalter (pp. 268–269) gives a brief index to themes in the Psalms. Note also that the reading of the Psalms is an integral part of the Lectionaries.

Chapter 12

Episcopal Services: The Ordinal

(BCP pp. 472–512)

The Anglican Church in North America is "episcopally ordered," i.e., bishops exercise the chief office in the governance and worship of the church. The section titled "Episcopal Services" brings together the Ordinal for ordaining deacons, priests and bishops (chapter 12); and two rites, one for installing ("instituting") a Rector and another for consecrating a church building (chapter 13).

PURPOSE

Lay people may wonder why such a "professional" initiation should be included in a book of *common* prayer. Good question. The answer is a profound one. The whole Church, clergy and laity, is called a royal priesthood and a holy nation (1 Peter 2:9). Hence no one may even be *considered* for ordination as a deacon or priest or to be consecrated a bishop unless a group of lay leaders in a local congregation such as yours, has first put the ball in play by recommending them for ordination. Just as you may hold this book in your hands, you or brothers and sisters dear to you will support and hold responsible a clergy person who has been ordained to serve in the life of the congregation.

Consider these words from the preface to the Ordinal:

> *No one shall be accounted to be a lawful Deacon, Priest or Bishop in this Church, or allowed to execute any of the said functions, without first being called, tried, examined, and admitted to such office according to the Form set forth in this book . . . The Bishop may only admit a candidate as a Deacon or Priest after sufficient examination and testing to determine that the candidate meets the requirements of the Canons, and is of virtuous conduct, without crime or impediment, instructed in the Holy Scriptures, and fit for ministry in Christ's Church.*

Just as a citizen is expected to obey those in authority, so also the citizen has a responsibility to choose elected officials wisely and hold them accountable for their actions.

The purpose of Holy Orders, the ordination of clergy, is to build up the Church as the Body of Christ by providing leaders who will nurture the growth of the Body through the sacraments, preach the Word of God, and enable every member of Christ's Body to reach out to those who need to see the Gospel lived out by the love and service of Christians.

The Church is truly Christ's Body on earth, and through the Church, God continues to nurture and love the world inside as well as outside the walls of church buildings. Each baptized Christian has been made an integral part of Christ's Body and has been given gifts from the Holy Spirit that are to be shared within the Body. Some are called to special ministries with special gifts, such as healing or hospitality. Others have gifts of service, administration, and helping; and some are called to the clergy.

CHARACTERISTICS

We must begin by understanding what a "call" to ordination is. In the biblical sense, *three* separate calls are required: *the call of God*, which, as in the case of the Old Testament Prophets, is God's sovereign act; *the call of the Church*, when it seeks to identify leaders who have the spiritual gifts that will enable them to exercise a particular ministry needed by the Church; and *the inner sense of call* by individuals themselves, who must prayerfully consider whether their natural talents, education, and personal gifts will benefit the whole Body. The individual so moved then enters into a serious discernment process with several prayerful guides to see whether it is really God's call.

What was the practice of the Early Church? As the age of the original Apostles passed away, those who had been brought into the body through the Apostles' ministry were called and appointed to be their successors. By the end of the first century, the three "orders" of deacon, presbyter, and bishop were established, and Anglican orders continue very much the same today, patterned on the threefold order of the historic Church.

A bishop (from the Greek *episcopos,* meaning "overseer") is a man called from among the already ordained clergy to take on a leadership role over a number of congregations in a particular territory. The bishop teaches and encourages his local leaders to preach and teach. He interacts with other bishops in the councils of regional, national, and worldwide contexts to help to preserve the orthodoxy and unity of the whole Church. In a sense, he is also the pastor to the clergy under his charge; and it is the bishop who ordains others called to ordained ministry. He must be consecrated by at least three other bishops to ensure that the wider Church agrees to his calling. His job description is well defined at BCP 2019 pp. 507–508. [Note: The Anglican Church in North America does not ordain female bishops. It allows local option for dioceses to ordain or not to ordain female presbyters and deacons.]

A Presbyter (from the Greek *presbyteros* meaning "elder"), also known as a priest, is selected through the discernment of the local laity and is ordained by the bishop by the laying on of hands. A priest serves usually as the leader of a local congregation, who preaches and teaches, administers the sacraments, and leads worship and has the spiritual care of the people in the local congregation. Priests cannot ordain or confirm others nor consecrate holy oils or church buildings, but they bless and pray with and for their flock.

Deacons (from the Greek *diakonos* meaning "servant") are mentioned in the Book of Acts, where they are described as those who "serve at tables" and care for the "widow, the orphan, the stranger." A deacon is ordained by the bishop alone, because the deacon is directly responsible to the bishop, rather than to any particular parish or priest.

The office of deacon is a unique calling of its own and not always a stepping stone to the priesthood. To distinguish people called to be permanent deacons (as opposed to priests-in-training who serve as deacons for a year) the terms used to distinguish among deacons now are "permanent deacon" and "transitional deacon."

By the end of the third century, Christian presbyters began to be compared in certain respects to the Old Testament priesthood, but the ordination service speaks primarily of their pastoral role as ministers of the Word and Sacraments.

Presbyters were the usual celebrants of the local community's Eucharist and took on the shepherding and teaching roles once held by the Apostles. It was clear that the presbyter was subordinate to the bishop and had no specific function when the bishop presided, unlike the deacon, who had a particular ongoing role with the bishop.

It is noteworthy that those ordained always retain the orders they received, from deacon to bishop. This is important, because ordination is permanent, just as Baptism is permanent. Thus a bishop continues being a priest, a deacon, and a baptized layperson.

A WALK THROUGH THE ORDINAL

The ordination rites for the three orders follow the same outline, but the readings, exhortations, and examinations and duties differ according to the nature and responsibilities of each order. The Ministry of the Word for all three Orders is much the same. The candidates are presented to the bishop or archbishop to subscribe "without reservation" to the "Oath of Conformity," to the Scriptures as God's Word, to the Thirty-Nine Articles of Religion and the doctrines presented in the BCP, and to an "Oath of Canonical Obedience." The bishop or archbishop then asks for the assembly's affirmation.

The process is not a mere formality; it is intended to reveal any doubts or misunderstandings a candidate might have, and spells out all the usual duties inherent in each role. The Exhortation for a candidate to the priesthood is much longer and pastoral than the other exhortations, in part because the burden of responsibility for the local congregation falls to the priest.

The Examination varies somewhat for each rite, but in general the candidates are asked to confirm that they are called to this ministry; that they believe Scripture contains all things necessary for salvation through faith in Jesus Christ; and that they are willing and able to undertake their ministry.

In The Ordination of a Priest, the *Veni, Creator Spiritus,* an ancient compilation of Biblical passages related to the work of the Holy Spirit, is sung or said. It is a prayer for the renewal of the Church with the candidate kneeling or prostrate. The bishop then consecrates the person, and the bishop and any attending priests lay hands on the head of the ordained to receive the Order of Priesthood. The newly ordained priest then celebrates the Eucharist with the bishop, delivers the bread to the people, and may lead the Post-Communion prayer. The blessing is by the bishop, and the dismissal is by a deacon.

The Consecration of a bishop is presided over by the archbishop as chief consecrator. The rite also requires at least three bishops to lay on hands, representing the unity of the College of Bishops in the governance of the Church. The Exhortation delivered by the archbishop outlines the duties of the office, quoting Scripture, "that we should not be hasty in laying hands and admitting any person to authority in the Church of Christ." As with the Ordination to the Priesthood, the Exhortation and Examination are followed by the *Veni, Creator Spiritus*.

APPLICATION

The ordination service is solemn, one might say awesome, but it must be remembered that salvation is not mediated through any deacon, priest, bishop, or archbishop; rather, our salvation depends solely on our relationship with Jesus Christ, the one Mediator between God and man, and his work on the Cross (1 Timothy 2:5). Further, there is such a thing as an order of the laity, to which we are "appointed" as members of his Body as is stated clearly in Scripture (1 Corinthians 12:12-27) and the canons of our Church "Concerning Laity":

> *The effective ministry of the Church is the responsibility of the laity no less than it is the responsibility of bishops and other clergy. It is incumbent for every lay member of the Church to become an effective minister of the gospel of Jesus Christ, one who is spiritually qualified, gifted, called, and mature in the faith.*

Chapter 13

Institution of a Rector and Consecration and Dedication of a Place of Worship

(BCP 2019 pp. 515–540)

W e address these rites together because both involve the bishop's oversight for all the churches in his diocese as the chief pastor, who delegates authority to ministers to lead his congregations, and who presides at both liturgies.

INSTITUTION OF A RECTOR: PURPOSE

While the titles and duties of Bishops, Priests and Deacons are firmly fixed in the Prayer Book, other clergy titles and duties vary from diocese to diocese. However, the office of Rector is the one consistent position exercised in a congregation. The word "institution," while somewhat archaic, captures the sense of fixed tenure and "right authority" granted to the Rector.

From the earliest days of the Church, a bishop has delegated his spiritual and canonical authority to ministers who lead congregations. A parish without an instituted Rector, or a mission church of the diocese, may have a minister who is designated by the bishop to be his vicar, often called the "deacon or priest in charge," who stands in the place of the bishop, and who is by canon law the official pastor of the congregation.

The purpose of the Institution of a Rector service is to welcome the new rector into the diocese and to introduce *him* to the congregation. (The italicized *he* or *him* in the service is generic. As noted above, diocesan canons in the ACNA regulate the role of women as deacons and priests, and only priests can be Rectors.) A Letter of Institution spells out the relationship of the Rector to his people, to the bishop, and to the diocese. It also admonishes the congregation to recognize the Rector's authority in leading and shepherding the people. Should there be any difficulty in the relationship of the Rector to the Vestry or the people, it is to be reported to the bishop, who is asked for his counsel. If the relationship is broken beyond repair, it is in the power of the bishop to revoke the minister's appointment.

The Rector must be a priest in good standing according to the qualfications of the ordination service and the canons of the diocese. His specific duties are spelled out in the Institution liturgy. The opening prayer outlines the responsibilities required in the office: authority to lead the congregation, that by holiness of life and sound preaching the new Rector will be of spiritual benefit to the flock. How is the Rector to do this? The presentation of Symbols of his office by representatives of the congregation the service demonstrate what is required:

Preach the Word (the Bible)
Administer the sacraments (bread and wine)
Be a person of prayer (the Book of Common Prayer)
Be a teacher of the faith (the Catechism)
Responsibility for what happens in the building (the keys)
Encourage missions and discipleship (baptismal water).

A WALK THROUGH THE SERVICE

The Institution may be performed as a service in its own right, but it usually continues with Holy Communion. The celebrant should be the bishop or his deputy representing the Diocese in the relationship of priest and parish.

The service begins with an Acclamation and the Collect for Purity. The wardens and new Rector come before the celebrant, and the wardens present the Rector. The celebrant reads out loud the Letter of Institution, and the Rector responds by recognizing the bishop's authority. The celebrant invites all assembled to join in saying or singing The Litany for Ordinations and concludes with a Collect. The lessons, a sermon, and the Nicene Creed follow.

The Presentation of the Symbols follows the Creed. The new Rector faces the celebrant, flanked by representatives of the congregation, as the symbols are presented. The new Rector then kneels and prays the Prayer of Dedication to God, to his call, and to his new congregation. (It is a prayer every Rector should pray often on their knees, right in the middle of the worship space.)

A new pastor, especially if new to the diocese and or to the community, will need the immediate support and fellowship of the members of the congregation, who should pray daily for the ministry and family of the rector, and tell the Rector that they are doing so.

Consecration and Dedication of a Place of Worship

The setting apart of holy space was important for the Old Testament people of God, and as the Church grew in the early centuries, church buildings were consecrated for worship.

Consecration of a worship space is a matter for the bishop and the mission of the whole diocese. For this reason, the bishop presides at the service. The Rector or minister in charge takes part as indicated. At the discretion of the bishop, neighboring ministers may be invited to participate and may be assigned appropriate parts in the liturgy.

The liturgy provides for the consecration and dedication not only of a Place of Worship but also of its furnishings. Places that may be set apart include purpose-built church structures, as well as facilities acquired and renovated for long-term use by a worshiping community. A Place of Worship may be consecrated and dedicated even if it is leased or mortgaged, provided the congregation has exclusive control of the facility, and to the extent the bishop and local canons allow. The liturgy does not preclude the use of the Place of Worship for educational, evangelical or social purposes, or other activities that give glory to God and help build up the Church.

Shared-use facilities like school auditoriums or community centers are not consecrated and dedicated, but *weekly* preparation for worship may include spiritual cleansing (exorcising) of any forces of darkness that may have entered, whether invited or uninvited.

It is desirable that all members of the congregation, young and old, have some individual or collective part in the celebration, as well as the architect, builders, musicians, artists, benefactors, and friends. If the church is also to be used for regular worship by other Christian bodies, it is most appropriate that their representatives also take part in the service.

When the clergy and people assemble before the service, they may gather out of doors or in some other building. When convenient, the procession may go around the facility to be dedicated, and then go to the principal door. Hymns or psalms may be used in procession, and the use of portable musical instruments is suitable.

When a new church is being consecrated, it may be desirable that sacred vessels, ornaments, and decorations be carried into the building in the procession. Such things as the deed for the property, the blueprint of the building, the keys, and the tools used in its construction may also be carried as well. Selected verses of psalms, hymns or instrumental music may be used as the ministers move from one part of the church to another.

If the place of public worship is also to serve as a school or parish hall, or for some other suitable purpose, the liturgy may be adapted to the circumstances, with the bishop's permission.

The Prayer Book (pp. 538-540) also provides a form for secularizing a facility previously used as a Place of Worship, when the use of the building for worship, or for the ministry of the congregation, has ended.

Chapter 14

Collects and Occasional Prayers

(BCP 2019 pp. 598–683)

PURPOSE

An integral part of one's own spiritual formation is to learn how God can use prayers that we have heard over and over again to speak directly to us, just as he does with Psalms and hymns. It works the other way around too. Prayers that have stood the test of time, and are rich in Biblical imagery, can assist us in learning to pray and in our daily devotions. In short, the Holy Spirit prompts us with holy words and images so that we can hear God's voice speaking to us, and as a result show us how we can respond in the same "language."

A Collect is a short and concentrated prayer that has a particular form and is a fundamental tool for the worship of God in the Anglican Way. Collects are usually addressed to God the Father, through the intercession of Jesus, and by the power of the Holy Spirit working within us. Collects in public prayer are a valuable means of calling us to focus on a theme or a passage that ties together our public and private prayers. In our private devotions, Collects are a good way to get us started by "priming the pump," so to speak.

BACKGROUND

Nothing ties Anglicans more firmly to the historic church than the Collect. Many of the Collects in the BCP 2019 are at least 1,500 years old and the product of the experiences of thousands of saints throughout the history of the Church. The earliest surviving collection of liturgies includes a series of Collects to be used at the Eucharist. The celebrant "collected" the individual prayers into a unifying conclusion.

Thomas Cranmer composed at least twenty-five Collects of his own for the 1549 BCP. The BCP 2019 has restored the ordering of the Collects as found in the 1662 BCP (still the most widely used Prayer Book worldwide) with the intention of reestablishing the Collects as a source for the people's recollection well beyond Sunday services.

CHARACTERISTICS

Just as a sonnet or a Japanese haiku have a certain metrical shape, a Collect (like Cranmer's famous Scripture Collect below—see BCP 2019 p. 598) has a particular form too, consisting of these five parts:

1. INVOCATION   An address to God that acknowledges his care for us:
   Blessed Lord,

2. ASCRIPTION   An action of God relevant to the prayer:
   Who caused all Holy Scriptures to be written for our learning:

3. PETITION   The request made in the prayer:
   Grant us to hear them, read, mark, learn, and inwardly digest them,

4. Intention   The purpose of the prayer:

   That by patience and the comfort of your holy Word we may embrace and ever hold fast the blessed hope of everlasting life,

5. Trinitarian Mediation and Amen   The closing:

   Which you have given us in our Savior Jesus Christ, who lives and reigns with you and the Holy Spirit, one God, for ever and ever. Amen.

A WALK THROUGH THE COLLECTS

The Collects of the Church Year have two main divisions. The Temporal series (BCP 2019 pp. 598–622) follows the Church Year in a regular progression from Advent to Epiphany and from Ash Wednesday to Trinity Sunday. The Sundays outside of these two cycles are called *Ordinary Time*. The Sanctoral series (BCP 2019 pp. 624–633) consists of the saints' days that were included in the original 1549 BCP Calendar.

APPLICATION

To whom do you pray?
How often do you consciously pray?
Why do you pray?

These are important questions to ask yourself! First of all, we are praying to personal Being, the living God, and not a "force" or a Santa Claus. Christians pray to the Father, by means of the Son, as encouraged by the Holy Spirit. But it doesn't matter which Person of the Trinity you address; you will be heard.

The second question is harder to answer for most of us because we are so hurried and harried by our lifestyles. Conscious praying requires three things: a quiet place, a quieted mind, and a willing heart. The third question is easy to answer, but hard to accomplish—the real reason to pray is for us to be present with

God, not to get God to give us something. Remember that God knows what we need before we ask. God doesn't need information from us; he wants *attention* from us.

Praying is similar to physical training in that it takes time and effort to overcome distractions and other obstacles so that we can give God our full attention. It often helps to turn to the Prayer Book for prayers that you can use as "starters" to get you focused, including the Occasional Prayers and the Collects.

It also takes patience to keep up the discipline when you "just don't feel like it." Patience is important for another reason: God is always trying to get our attention, but we are often too preoccupied and impatient to wait long enough to hear God, who whispers "in a still, small voice." God deserves our patience and persistence to become aware of the gifts he showers on us. A particularly helpful Scripture to memorize in this context is Romans 12:12, "Rejoice in hope, be patient in tribulation, be constant in prayer."

A collection of "Occasional Prayers" follows the Collects. "Occasional" can be a word that doesn't require much attention, but you need to know about this section of the Prayer Book. It contains time-honored prayers and thanksgivings that comport with Holy Scripture. You will find the 125 Occasional Prayers organized by Content (pp. 642–645), including The Church; Creation; The Nation (USA or Mexico and Canada); Society; Those in Need; Family and Personal LIfe; Personal Devotion; At Times of Prayer and Worship; Death, the Departed and the Communion of Saints; and Thanksgivings. Many prayers are anonymous, but some are by famous saints of the Church, such as Francis of Assisi, John Wesley, Thomas Aquinas, and Julian of Norwich.

There will be times where you will draw strength from these offerings or need them to help jump-start your prayers.

Chapter 15

The Church Year: Special Liturgies, Calendars, and Lectionaries

(BCP 2019 pp. 543–595, 687–763)

PURPOSE

The next main section of the Prayer Book is dedicated to the Church Year. Why have a Church Year? The uniqueness of our faith is that *God participates in our lives through time.* Through our baptism we become members within a family history that has a beginning—God's creation; a middle—where we are now; and an ending—the consummation of all things in Jesus's return. The heart of the Gospel is the good news of God's self-revelation in time and in space by the life, death, and resurrection of Jesus Christ.

The purpose of the Church Year is to keep us in continual relationship, in our time and space, with the eternal and universal redemptive purposes of God as revealed in Jesus Christ, to enable us to participate with the One whose we are.

The Church Year gives us landmarks whereby we participate in the historic reality of the life and ministry of Jesus, learn of our relationship to Jesus's family of faith down through human history, and come to know the hope that we share in God's redemption of all he has created and continues to love unconditionally.

CHARACTERISTICS

The Calendar of the Church Year consists of two great parts: the Christmas (Incarnation) Cycle from Advent through Epiphany, and the Easter (Paschal) Cycle from Ash Wednesday to the Day of Pentecost. The remainder of the Year is called the Season "after Pentecost" or the Trinity Season (Trinitytide) and extends until the day before Advent begins.

The climax of the Paschal Cycle comes during the forty days of Lent, culminating in Holy Week and Easter. For this reason, there is a series of "Special Liturgies" capped by the Great Vigil of Easter. There are special liturgies of Lent and Holy Week at BCP 2019 pp. 543–595. These are easy to read and understand, so we needn't delve into to them here, except to call them to your attention by naming them: ASH WEDNESDAY—PALM SUNDAY—MAUNDY THURSDAY—GOOD FRIDAY—HOLY SATURDAY—THE GREAT VIGIL OF EASTER

There is also a schedule of Holy Days and commemorations of Christian saints, whose lives manifested the presence of the Holy Spirit by emulating Jesus's life in their own lives. This Calendar is followed by tables for finding the date of Easter and other moveable dates.

Lectionaries

PURPOSE

The BCP 2019 states on p. 716, "The public reading of Scripture in the liturgies of the Church is among the most important features of any act of worship." We now live in circumstances where even regular churchgoers show a profound ignorance of the Bible and what it says. How can we know the Lord's will if we never listen to what he has had to say to us? Daily meditation on the Word of God is an essential component of every Christian's life.

The Lectionaries (BCP 2019 pp. 716–763) are simply lists of the Scripture readings assigned for a particular day. The ACNA Prayer Book has two separate Lectionary cycles: one for the celebration of the Eucharist, and the other for the readings for the Daily Office. The Eucharistic Lectionary for Sundays covers the content of the four Gospels in three years. The Daily Office Lectionary provides us a ready guide for traveling the entire length of the Bible in one year.

As Christians, we read the Bible, both the Old and New Testaments, through a Christian lens that interprets what we read from a specific viewpoint. As the Catechism explains, "The Old Testament is to be read in the light of Christ, incarnate, crucified, and risen; and the New Testament is to be read in light of God's revelation to Israel." Together, both Testaments are Holy Scripture, telling a unified story of God and his people.

CHARACTERISTICS

As noted in the Preface, "the Prayer Book is just the Bible organized for public worship." Indeed, 90 percent of the words in BCP 2019 are direct quotations of Scripture; the rest are canticles and prayers that go back some 1,500 years, while its New Coverdale Psalter is rooted in the Great Bible of the sixteenth century. Our Prayer Book derives from an intentional attempt to allow the people to recognize the same texts, whether in the Bible or BCP, and thereby to make the texts more readily memorable.

BACKGROUND

In antiquity, the Jews in their synagogue worship read the *Torah* scroll (the Pentateuch) all the way through once every year. Jesus inaugurated his public ministry by attending his home synagogue at Nazareth (Luke 4:16–21). When the synagogue elders asked him to read, he selected the scroll containing the prophet Isaiah (61:1–2).

The Early Church discerned that the Holy Spirit was active in the writing of the Scriptures; that Scriptures were "God-breathed" (2 Timothy 3:16). The Old Testament expresses God's Covenant with the people of Israel, and Jesus's death and resurrection seals a New Covenant with those who profess his name.

From the Early Church onward, the Old Testament was read in relation to the appointed Gospel for the day. The Church saw that many of the people and events found in the New Testament were clearly foreshadowed in the Old Testament. Similarly, the New Testament reading would be chosen to relate in some way to the Gospel.

At the time of the Great Reformation, the innovation of movable type revolutionized printing, and books became more affordable to anyone to who could read; the Bible was now available to all people. But since less than half of the laity could read, Archbishop Cranmer took great care in finding ways for the Scriptures to be publicly read every day in the local church.

While his Eucharistic lectionary remained traditional, his lectionary for the Divine Office was radically new and very comprehensive: the entire Bible was to be read through in one year, with two Old Testament and two New Testament readings and a portion of the Psalter read each day. Anglicans arriving in North America in Colonial times used the BCP exactly as it was used in England. In creating the BCP 2019, the ACNA College of Bishops determined that, following Cranmer's lead, the whole of the Bible should be read in one year for the Daily Office, and the entire New Testament within the three-year Eucharistic Cycle.

A WALK THROUGH THE LECTIONARIES

Sunday and Holy Days

The Church Year begins on the first Sunday in Advent, which falls in late November or early December. There are three cycles of readings for successive years. Year A begins on the first Sunday of Advent (Advent 1) in years that are divisible by three. The chart that begins on BCP 2019 p. 717 has four columns: the Day of the Church Year is on the left, and columns for Year A (Matthew), Year B (Mark) and Year C (Luke) list the Old Testament, Psalm, New Testament, and Gospel readings assigned for the day. These continue through Advent (4 weeks), Christmas (12 days), Epiphany (up to 9 weeks), Lent (6 weeks), Holy Week, and Eastertide (7 weeks).

The Gospel readings for the season after Pentecost and until the end of the Church Year focus on what Jesus taught, rather than on his life from birth to resurrection. This time-frame has no events in it, so the Sundays are numbered from Pentecost onward as "2nd Sunday after Pentecost," etc. Pentecost will not fall on the same day each year, so to make things simpler, the term *Proper* is used for the readings, which refers to what the "proper" lessons are for that Sunday.

In addition to the Gospel and Old Testament, the lectionaries include extended readings from the Epistles of the New Testament. It is important that clergy integrate the whole corpus of Biblical texts in their preaching.

Within the Church Year are days that may be celebrated on a weekday, such as saints' commemorations, Ember Days, and

National Days. These and the Holy Days on pp. 730–731 also have Propers provided for the celebration of the Eucharist.

The Daily Office Lectionary

The explanation of how to follow the scheduled readings for the Daily Office begins on BCP 2019 p. 734. In general, readings move continuously through the books of the Bible, interrupted only by Holy Days. The first lesson is from the Old Testament (on occasion, a reading from the Apocrypha may be provided). The Gospels and Acts of the Apostles are read through twice in the year, and the other parts of the New Testament are also read twice, except for the Book of Revelation, which is read once in Advent.

If four readings each day is difficult to accomplish, the rubrics provide a way to make the readings a two-year cycle instead.

Modern computer technology also provides several complete sets of readings and Psalms at our fingertips. While it is important to know something about the lectionaries, and how they work to support the Church Year, you needn't struggle through them by yourself. Now if you wish you can go online to read the Daily Office each day.

APPLICATION

The Bible is God's Word. It is not an encyclopedia with lists of information, nor is it simply a collection of poetry and stories. Our biblical texts cover several millennia and have one thing in common: they are the record of what God has done through human history and what God inspired the Prophets and Apostles to say to his people. And these are *living words*, not dead letters; they speak to us in our personal situations. We have stressed in some detail the importance of the daily reading of Scripture as integral to the devotional life. Owning and using your own Bible is essential. There is a variety of sizes and formats you may choose from. There are also many good translations. The ACNA College of Bishops has preferred the English Standard Version (ESV), as it follows the principle of careful translation of words and phrases from the original languages of Scripture. This method goes back to William Tyndale (1494–1536), whose translation of the Bible into English cost him his life.

Archbishop Cranmer left us the memorable Scripture Collect that urges us to "read, mark, learn, and inwardly digest" God's Word. We are used to skimming while we read, which is fine for some things, but not for Scripture. If it is truly God's Word written, it deserves the time and effort to read it slowly and carefully. Your author reads it aloud to himself to keep from going too fast or letting his mind wander.

Begin with a short prayer, asking the Holy Spirit to guide you in your reading. As you read it verse by verse, when something jumps out at you, stay with the verse and "chew" on it. Ask God why this strikes you—what is God trying to say to you personally? Keep a pad or notebook with you, write down those passages that strike you as important, and go back and reflect on them during the day. After a week or so, look over the verses you have written down, and ask yourself some questions, such as: Is there a pattern or repeated theme in what I have written down? Are there other passages that relate to this one? Look up words or find parallel verses.

Ask God to open your eyes to see what is behind the words and phrases. You will even find that a verse you had thought you understood suddenly takes on a deeper meaning you hadn't known was there. The Holy Spirit does that sort of thing!

Chapter 16

Documentary Foundations

(BCP 2019 pp. 766–802)

The BCP 2019 includes Foundational Documents to help Anglicans understand the concepts and decisions that have formed the basis of our Church and our faith. They are not light reading, but they are well worth reviewing to help understand the background for Anglicanism in general, and that of our Anglican Church in North America in particular. You will come away with the understanding that we are not so much a "denomination" as we are a bridge back to the Apostolic Faith of the Early Church and forward to the English Reformation and Anglican Communion. You will find these documents, sometimes called "formularies," are rich in content.

THE FUNDAMENTAL DECLARATIONS OF THE PROVINCE— CONCERNING THE NICENE CREED—THE ATHANASIAN CREED—THE THIRTY-NINE ARTICLES OF RELIGION— THE JERUSALEM DECLARATION—THE PREFACE OF THE BOOK OF COMMON PRAYER (1549) AND (1662)

Fundamental Declarations of the Province

(BCP 2019 p. 766)

These begin with this foundational statement:

> *As the Anglican Church in North America (the Province), being a part of the One, Holy, Catholic, and Apostolic Church of Christ, we believe and confess Jesus Christ to be the Way, the Truth, and the Life: no one comes to the Father but by Him.*

There follows a statement of seven elements that are "characteristic of the Anglican Way, and essential for membership":

> *That the Old and New Testaments are the inspired Word of God.*
>
> *That Baptism and the Eucharist are Sacraments ordained by Christ himself.*
>
> *That the hierarchical structure of Anglican polity, the historic Episcopate, is an inherent part of apostolic faith and practice and integral to our unity.*
>
> *That the three Catholic Creeds and teaching of the first four Councils and Christological clarifications of the fifth, sixth, and seventh Councils are authoritative "in so far as they are agreeable to the Holy Scriptures."*
>
> *We affirm the decisions that resulted from seven Councils of the undivided Church.*
>
> *That The* Book of Common Prayer *is our standard for Anglican doctrine and discipline.*
>
> *That the Thirty-Nine Articles of Religion, while rooted in its historic context, express fundamental principles of authentic Anglican belief.*

Concerning the Nicene Creed

(BCP 2019 p. 768)
The Nicene Creed is not reproduced here but appears on several occasions in the Prayer Book, most importantly in the Eucharistic liturgies. The series of Resolutions by the ACNA College of Bishops found on this page addresses an historic division between Eastern and Western churches over the confession that the Holy Spirit proceeds "from the Father and the Son."

The Athanasian Creed

(BCP 2019 pp. 768–771)
The Athanasian Creed is the most thoroughgoing statement of the doctrine of the Holy Trinity and the Person of Jesus Christ as true God and true Man. It warns against falling away from the Catholic Faith of the historic Church.

The Thirty-Nine Articles of Religion

(BCP 2019 pp. 772–790)
The Thirty-Nine Articles of Religion (1571) is the confession of faith produced by the Church of England at the time of the Reformation and since then have been included in Anglican Prayer Books worldwide. This confession, while archaic and its language and some of its concerns, remains the normative teaching of the Anglican Communion. One of the fundamentals of the Articles is its commitment to the authority of the Bible as "God's word written" and as containing "all things necessary to salvation" (Articles 6 and 20).

The Jerusalem Declaration

(BCP 2019 pp. 791–793)

The Anglican Church in North America is part of a worldwide fellowship of Anglicans which began with the formation of the Anglican Communion in 1867. The Anglican Communion has represented eighty million Anglican Christians on every continent, the majority of whom are from the Global South.

In 2008 the Global Anglican Future Conference (GAFCON) was convened in Jerusalem to deal with a departure from the biblical faith in several Western churches, including the Episcopal Church USA and Anglican Church of Canada. In its Conference Statement, the Gafcon churches invited the confessing churches in North America to be recognized, and in 2009 the Anglican Church in North America was formed.

The first Conference also produced a confession of faith, the Jerusalem Declaration, which articulates a "mere Anglicanism" that unites its member churches. The Jerusalem Declaration among other items states:

> *We rejoice in our Anglican sacramental and liturgical heritage as an expression of the gospel, and we uphold the 1662 Book of Common Prayer as a true and authoritative standard of worship and prayer, to be translated and locally adapted for each culture.*

The Anglican Church in North America has adopted the Jerusalem Declaration as a true statement of Anglican identity.

Preface of the 1549 and 1662 Books of Common Prayer

(BCP 2019, pp. 794–802)

Despite tumults over the centuries, the BCP as we know it has survived for very close to 500 years without significant changes. Reading the early Prefaces can give you a sense of the "why" of that.

The Anglican Church in North America sees itself as standing in this historic tradition. Here is a quotation from the Preface of the BCP 2019 (pp. 1-5):

> The Book of Common Prayer (2019) *is indisputably true to Cranmer's originating vision of a form of prayers and praises that is thoroughly biblical, catholic in the manner of the early centuries, highly participatory in delivery, peculiarly Anglican and English in its roots, culturally adaptive and missional in a most remarkable way, utterly accessible to the people, and whose repetitions are intended to form the faithful catechetically and to give them doxological voice.*

About the Author

The career of the Rev. Dr. Arnold W. Klukas covers a wide and rich service of Christ, which included a B.A. in History (Wittenberg University), a M.Div. (Yale Divinity School), a Ph.D. (University of Pittsburgh).

Worship traditions and ascetical practices have been a lifelong passion with Father Klukas. Nearly equal to his religious passion has been his fascination with architectural history and religious art. All these interests were encouraged while he was an undergraduate at Wittenberg University: would it be teaching art and architecture, or church ministry.

He chose Yale Divinity School where, to his dismay, he found neither worship nor the practice of spiritual disciplines were of importance. A fellowship to study theology at Oxford University provided an escape from the trendy liberal scene—and into the Anglican tradition.

A National Endowment for the Humanities Fellowship to do his research in Great Britain led to a curacy in London at All Saints, Margaret Street, where he found his dual vocation of the priesthood and teaching. Returning to the USA in 1978, he taught art history at Oberlin and Smith colleges.

His priestly life won out, however, and he began fifteen years of parish ministry in Pittsburgh, where by God's grace he was able to revitalize a dying inner-city parish into a dynamic center for Anglo-Catholic worship and spirituality, a flourishing arts ministry, a multifaceted social outreach to the neighborhood, and a mission church that soon outgrew its "mother" in size.

In 2002 Father Klukas came to Nashotah House Seminary as a Professor of Linguistics and Ascetical Theology. At Nashotah House, he found his job "made in Heaven" where his dual vocations as a scholar-teacher were combined into one job in one location.

Father Klukas retired from Nashotah in 2013 and continues to be actively engaged in the life of the Anglican Church in North America, where he is a member of the Task Force on Liturgy and leads retreats and workshops.

Printed in the USA
CPSIA information can be obtained
at www.ICGtesting.com
LVHW062127131223
766140LV00079B/1405